Five Days
That Shook
The World

Seattle and Beyond

Five Days
That Shook the World

Seattle and Beyond

◆

ALEXANDER COCKBURN

AND

JEFFREY ST. CLAIR

◆

PHOTOGRAPHS BY
ALLAN SEKULA

VERSO
London • New York

First published by Verso 2000
© Alexander Cockburn and Jeffrey St. Clair 2000
All rights reserved

VERSO
UK: 6 Meard Street, London WIV 3HR
USA: 180 Varick Street, 10th Floor, New York, NY 10014-4606

Verso is the imprint of New Left Books

ISBN 1 85984 779 X

British Library Cataloguing in Publication Data
A catalogue record for this book is available from the British Library

Library of Congress Cataloging-in-Publication Data
A catalog record for this book is available from the Library of Congress

Typeset in Stemple Schneidler by Total Graphics, Skokie, IL
Printed in the United Kingdom
October 2000

Contents

1   The New Movement   1

2   Seattle Diary   13

3   Who Won?   53

4   DC Diaries   70

5   LA Diary   87

6   The Jackboot State   100

7   What Are We Fighting For?   113

The authors wish to thank

The Fund for Constitutional Government

for its grant in support of this book.

Chapter 1

The New Movement

What we saw in Seattle across those tumultuous days stretching from November 28 through December 3, 1999, and then in Davos, Switzerland, Washington DC, Philadelphia, Los Angeles and Prague was the flowering of a new radical movement in America and across the world, rambunctious, anarchic, internationalist, well informed and in some ways more imaginative and supple than kindred popular eruptions in recent decades.

After the initial rout of the WTO in Seattle many in this new movement didn't always comprehend the extent of their victory. Five months later, some demonstrators in Washington DC across the weekend April 15–17, 2000 grumbled about press coverage of "A16" suggesting that they had "failed" in their efforts to close down the World Bank talks in the nation's capital and that therefore the Seattle momentum was sputtering to a halt. These protesters were missing the full depth of their triumph: namely that they had managed to place their issues squarely on the national and indeed global political agenda.

A decade, even five years ago, officials of the World Bank and International Monetary Fund were florid with righteous self satisfaction at the good works their institutions were performing round the world. By the spring of 2000 these same officials were apologizing for the sins of their past and nervously contending that they are re-engineering themselves as forces for good. It was the same on the sweatshop issue. Hardly a month goes by, without a firm like Nike edgily advertising its efforts to be responsive to the charges of critics about pay scales and labor practices in the Third World.

Take a look at some of the threads in this new activist, populist movement. Start with the Ruckus Society, one of whose founders is Mike Roselle, a man whose political lineage goes back to Abbie Hoffman's Yippies, to a grounding in progressive politics and then to Earth First!, which he co-founded with Dave Foreman. Roselle had long argued that large-scale, non-violent civil disobedience could shut down a city and take over the theme shows organized by world capital, such as the WTO conference in Seattle.

The Yippies understood political drama and so do the Ruckusites and the Anarchists. They also understand fun.

Add to this brew of militant environmentalism and sense of street theater the concerns of the anti-globalization crowd for economic justice. In thirty minutes worth of speeches in the Ellipse in Washington DC on April 16 one could hear speakers talk about sweatshops, cancellation of Third World debt, the menace of bio-technology, unequal exchange in world trade, labor organizing at the global level. One criticism of the rallies and marches outside the Democratic convention in Los Angeles was that there were so many — against sweatshops, Iraq sanctions, the Ramparts police division, the death sentence on Mumia abu Jamal, Occidental's oil leases on U'wa lands in Colombia (to name only a few) that perhaps energies were excessively scattered.

One issue flows into another, as the Berkeley-based International Rivers Network discovered years ago. As the IRN battled dams around the world, it found that dams mostly had one thing in common: financial backing from the World Bank. So the IRN founded the enormously effective "50 Years Is Enough" campaign against the Bank.

In the same way, defenders of forests around the world found themselves looking at forest-destroying agricultural programs backed by the World Bank, also at "austere structural adjustment" programs imposed on Third World countries by the IMF.

As with all new radical movements, some of the bloodlines go back a long way, to movements of Third World solidarity that started in the 1960s and earlier. The anti-NAFTA battles of the early 1990s gave birth to organizations such as the Naderite Citizens Trade Campaign, highly visible both in Seattle and Washington.

There's a new student activism too, markedly different from the gender and identity concerns of the early 1990s. Across America campuses are being organized by Students United Against Sweatshops, bringing in speakers from UNITE, Jeff Ballinger's Press for Change and Global Exchange.

What's different about this new movement? It's anti-corporate, but in a manner far more specific than older railings about "international capital". We live in the age of the brand name, and so we see well-informed campaigns against specific companies — Nike, Boise Cascade, Monsanto. It's well informed and internationalist, a tribute to the powers of the internet. In America, as evidenced by the large protests at both conventions in August, 2000, it's antagonistic to both the Republican and Democratic Parties. As yet this movement has not produced a new generation of leaders, and this is perhaps no bad thing, at least in the eyes of those who endured the ego-tripping of earlier times. It's less sexist too, and rich in ethnic diversity.

People are always declaring the left to be dead. No less an authority than Perry Anderson, editor of New Left Review, declared in that journal in the spring of 2000 that "the only starting-point for a realistic Left today is a lucid registration of historical defeat". Anderson wrote with gloomy relish: "For the first time since the Reformation there are no longer any significant oppositions—that is, systematic rival outlooks—within the thought-world of the West; and scarcely any on a world scale either."

We were reading those plangent lines as news came over the radio of a tree-sit in a section of the Headwaters redwood forest, in Humboldt County, northern California. A young woman called Firebird, fresh up from San Francisco, was tree-sitting forty feet up in the air. She'd fixed a rope with a noose round her neck, with the other end tied to a gate on the ground.

If the loggers or their allies launched an attack, Firebird was in imminent danger of being hanged. Firebird represents the will and courage of the new radical movement. In Anderson's terms, she represents a significant opposition within the official thought-world of the West, as did Hazel Wolf, a 101-year militant in Seattle with roots extending back through years of work setting up branches of the Audubon society throughout the Pacific Northwest to organizing in the Communist Party in the 1930s. Wolf died a few weeks after the Battle of Seattle which she had planned to attend.

In the heady days after the WTO demonstrations in Seattle, the question on everyone's lips was: where do we go from here? How do we sustain the movement? This presented the greatest hurdle to long-term coalition-building. How, for example, were French farmers supposed to remain in solidarity with Teamsters from Tacoma? Others veterans of the street battles of Seattle could see the diversity and unpredictability of the uprising against the WTO as its prime virtue.

In the end, as was inevitable, efforts to capitalize on the momentum of Seattle advanced on multiple fronts and showed the extent of the overall coalition. Global Trade Watch, a Ralph Nader-sponsored operation, was responsible for many of the planned events during WTO week in Seattle, including lectures, NGO tribunals, debates and several protests. Post-Seattle they proposed the "Fix It or Nix It Campaign," a plan to keep the pressure on the WTO.

One of the big issues for the CTC and big labor was China's potential entry into the WTO. "All the energy and momentum from Seattle is going directly into a huge national campaign to block permanent most-favored-nation status for China", proclaimed Lori Wallach, director of Global TradeWatch.. "The people at the Seattle rallies have gone home bolstered by their success and they are looking for their next fight. Members of Congress had better be prepared to find hundreds of trade activists camped out at their district offices."

Opposition to China's admission to the WTO (an opposition viewed with considerable reserve by the present authors) was only one of ten items on a list of demands that Global Trade Watch activists had come up with. Among the others: abolish the WTO trade-related intellectual property agreement; restore each nation's right to make its own decisions about goods sold in its domestic markets; allow individual nations to set their own environmental and health standards; exclude water and biological life forms from any trade rule applications.

The Campaign would give the WTO 18 months to make these changes or, according to a memo by Darci Anderssen, "we will launch campaigns worldwide to both cut off our countries' WTO funding contributions and to get our countries out of WTO". But there was a potential divide here between those talking about reform of the WTO and those who opposed its very existence. "The momentum coming out of Seattle was toward a global campaign to kill the WTO", Michael Donnelly, an environmental organizer from Salem, Oregon who has twice run for congress as a Green, told us early in 2000. "The WTO is a star chamber for the global capitalists. It will never serve the interests of working people or the environment. It can't be fixed."

Donnelly argued that the real legacy of the WTO protests was the sense of optimism and renewed energy it infused into ongoing campaigns against corporate rapacity. An example was the fresh impetus given to the anti-bio-tech movement. Shortly after WTO in Seattle, the Food and Drug Administration held a hearing in Oakland on genetically engineered foods on December. More than a thousand people turned out to protest. It was the largest anti-biotech gathering to date in the United States. Ronnie Cummins, director of the PureFood Campaign, credited Seattle with providing the stimulus. "Seattle made people feel as if they had some power once again. As the Battle of Seattle showed, the entire World Trade Organization is now being undermined by a growing international alliance of Civil Society—consumers, farmers, workers, environmentalists, and young people. The most important lesson of Seattle is that there is now a global New Democracy Movement being built, from the grassroots up. Food safety and genetic engineering are clearly proving to be one of the strategic pressure points or weak spots of global corporate power."

Another movement that got a boost from Seattle was Jubilee 2000, the international campaign to cancel third world debt. Jubilee 2000 sponsored one of the more creative events in Seattle, an attempt to form a human chain around Paul Allen-financed expo center to keep WTO delegates from attending a soiree with corporate executives from Microsoft and Boeing. Thousands of people turned out amid fierce winds and rain. There Jubilee 2000 and the 50 Years Is Enough Campaign went on to plot a week of protests in Washington, DC against the activities of the finance mavens at the World Bank and International Monetary Fund.

But perhaps the most intriguing movement to emerge from Seattle was the Alliance for Sustainable Jobs and the Environment, a coalition of Earth First!ers and Steelworkers that come together early in 1999, but first made its presence felt on the streets of Seattle. This unlikely union was pulled together by two remarkable people, David Brower, founder of Friends of the Earth and Earth Island Institute , and David Foster, David Foster, director for District 11 of the United Steelworkers of America, one of the most articulate labor leaders in the country.

The Earth First!ers and the Steelworkers had a common enemy: Maxxam Corporation and its CEO, corporate raider Charles Hurwitz. Hurwitz had used his Houston-based Maxxam to plot the takeover of two other companies, Pacific Lumber and Kaiser Aluminum. Pacific Lumber owned the largest swath of redwoods in private hands and Maxxam's rampages after the takeover prompted years of protests and civil disobedience by Earth First!ers. Hurwitz's takeover of Kaiser was followed by the usual onslaught of cost-slashing and kindred attacks on workers, culminating in a lock-out of 3,000 Steelworkers at its plants in Washington, Ohio and Louisiana. "We came together because we found we had a common foe", Foster told us. "But that foe is more than Hurwitz. It's the kind of global capitalism that exploits both workers and the environment."

After its strong showing in Seattle, the Alliance joined with about 20 other groups in an effort to force presidential candidates to grapple with the issue of global trade. The first stage was "Raucus at the Caucus," a weeklong series of protests and events during the run-up to the Iowa Caucuses. The group developed a "people's challenge", prodding the candidates on issues ranging from logging on federal lands to protection of family farms and workers right to strike.

On the one hand, optimism. On the other hand, the need to be as radical as reality. By August of 2000, nine months after Seattle, it was clear in Los Angeles that people were sometimes losing sight on a basic point. Demonstrations flow out of organization and are only a tool in a political campaign or movement. Demonstrations didn't end the war in Vietnam. Demonstrations were only part, sometimes a small part, of long years of movement building and political campaigning at multiple levels. There can be a point when demonstrations achieve nothing, and if evident failures, are capable of demoralizing and trivializing any given campaign.

You can take the state by surprise only once or twice in a generation. May/June, 1968, took the French state by surprise. The French state then took very good care not have that unpleasant experience repeated. The same reaction by the state's security apparat happened after Seattle, which represented a terrible humiliation on a global stage for the US government. By the time of the April protest in Washington any talk of constitutional rights to assembly and protest was a joke.

In mid-June of 2000 John Jonik, an alert reader of our newsletter CounterPunch sent us a tiny legal notice in the ad section of the Philadelphia Inquirer for June 7. The box, in what looked like 6 point type, was headed "City of Philadelphia" and then on the next line, "Public Hearing on June 12, 2000, 12.00 p.m., Room 400, City Hall to hear testimony on the following item: An Ordinance amending Title 10 of the Philadelphia Code entitled 'Regulation of Individual Conduct and Activity' prohibiting concealed identities in certain instances. Immediately following the public hearing, a meeting of the Committee on Public Safety, open to the public, will be held to consider the action to be taken on the above listed item."

What we had here was preliminary clearing of the decks for the demonstrations expected to take place during the Republican convention in Philadelphia in July. Constitutional protections for free speech and assembly were to be swept aside, with police permitted to arrest anyone wearing ski masks, hooded sweatshirts, scarves, acting in a suspicious manner and so forth. As Jonik wryly asked, "Some women's hats include net veils. Included? Illegal in a demo? Are real beard legal and fake ones not? What about wigs and/or hair coloring, fake scars, tattoos and piercings? Big sunglasses?" And what about those big wearable puppet outfits which featured big in the anti-WTO demonstrations in Seattle and Washington?

The demonstrations in Seattle provoked complete hysteria in authorities in cities anticipating protests of this kind. In the late spring of 2000 Windsor, Ontario, right across the river from Detroit, hosted what turned out to be a demure meeting of 34 foreign ministers of the Organization of American States. All 2000 cops in Windsor were issued with gas masks. A brick road was tarmacked to prevent its old bricks being used as missiles. The venue of the scheduled talks was surrounded with a high fence. The other side of the river, 4,000 US police officers were on full alert. Naomi Klein, a very smart writer who recently published the first-class *No Logo: Taking Aim At The Brand Bullies,* about corporations like Nike, wrote a fierce column about the Windsor event for the Toronto Globe and Mail, pointing out that the citizenry was being firmly guided towards the view that public protest was somehow per se illegal, and properly dealt with by savage police violence. Constitutional protections were being automatically suspended and anyone preparing to participate in an entirely legal manner in a demonstration treated as though they are felonious terrorists.

Klein reported a graphic designer in Windsor getting preemptively hassled by cops in Windsor, just for making signs. She described meeting young demonstrators in Washington wearing goggles and bandannas soaked in vinegar, "not that they were planning to attack a Starbucks, just that they thought that getting gassed is what happens when you express your political views". Civil disobedience such as sit-ins, Klein correctly pointed out, was (and still is) now automatically equated by the cops, prosecutors and judges as "violence". Arrested in 1999 in Philadelphia for demonstrating near the Liberty Bell in support of Mumia abu Jamal and Leonard Peltier, a New York green named Mitchel Cohen and several others were convicted in US District Court of failing to obey the order of a Park Service officer. This is the sort of charge that usually gets dismissed a few days after a demonstration. Cohen and the others not only got fined $250 plus $25 to the victims' restitution fund, but also drew a year's probation, meaning the threat of warrantless searches, urine tests and so forth. Cohen also got his passport lifted. Another Abu Jamal organizer got a request from the FBI for ten years' worth of financial records.

The message of the state is clear enough. The only "good protesters" are those waving a couple of placards in a cop-designated parking lot four miles from downtown. All others are "bad demonstrators", targets for pepper spray, police bludgeons, wire taps, pre-emptive hassles and a very hard time in court if they have the audacity to contest whatever charges the local prosecutors lay on them. We haven't moved far from that infamous '68 police riot in Chicago against antiwar protesters out the Democratic convention. The only difference is that today in the press and on television there's scant outrage at these militarized assaults on the rights of free speech and assembly, part and parcel of a larger connivance by respectable opinion at the state's unrelenting attrition of the Bill of Rights.

Chapter 2

Jeffrey St. Clair's Seattle Diary: It's a Gas, Gas, Gas

Seattle has always struck me as a suspiciously clean city, manifesting a tidiness that verges on the compulsive. It is the Singapore of the United States: spit-polished, glossy, eerily beautiful. Indeed, there is, perhaps, no more scenic setting for a city: nestled next to Elliot Bay on Puget Sound, with the serrated tips of the Olympic Mountains on the western skyline and hulking over it all the cool blue hump of Mt. Rainier.

But Seattle is also a city that hides its past in the underground. It is literally built on layers of engineered muck, a soggy Ilium. The new opulence brought by the likes of Microsoft, Boeing, Starbucks and REI is neatly segregated from the old economic engines, the working docks, the steamy pulp mills and chemical plants of south Seattle and Tacoma. It is a city that is both uptight and laid back, a city of deeply repressed desires and rages. It was the best and the worst of places to convene the WTO, that Star Chamber for global capitalists. On this week Seattle was so tightly wound that it seemed primed to crack. The city, which practiced drills to prepare itself against possible biological or chemical warfare by WTO opponents, was about to witness its own police department gas its streets and neighborhoods. By the end of the week, much of Seattle's shiny veneer had been scraped off, the WTO talks had collapsed in futility and acrimony and a new multinational popular resistance had blackened the eyes of global capitalism and its shock troops, if only for a few raucous days and nights.

Sunday

I arrived in Seattle at dusk and settled into the King's Inn, my noisy little motel on Fifth Avenue two blocks up from the ugly Doric columns of the Westin, the HQ of the US trade delegation and on Tuesday and Wednesday nights the high-rise hovel of Bill Clinton. On the drive up from Portland, I had decided to forego the press briefings, NGO policy sessions and staged debates slated for dozens of venues around Seattle. Instead, I was determined to pitch my tent with the activists who had vowed months earlier to shut down Seattle during WTO week. Today, the plan seemed remotely possible. With its overburdened streets and constricted geography the city does half the job itself. And, in an act of self-interested solidarity, the cabbies, who held festering grudges against the city on a variety of claims, had announced plans to time a taxi strike to coincide with the protest.

Around 10 PM, I wandered down to the Speakeasy Café, in the Belltown District, which I'd heard was to be a staging area for grassroots greens and anarchists with modems. On this warm late November night, there were stars in the Seattle sky, surely a once a decade experience. I took it as an omen. God knows of what strange portent.

The Speakeasy is a fully-wired redoubt for radicals: it serves beer, herbal tea, vegan dishes and, for a $10 fee, access to a bank of computers where dozens of people checked their email and the latest news, from Le Monde to the BBC, from WTOwatch.com to the New York Times. I ran into Kirk Murphy, a doctor who teaches at the UCLA medical school. I'd gotten to know Murphy slightly during the great battles to fight DreamWorks and its ill-fated plan to bury the Ballona Wetlands in Los Angeles under acres of concrete, glass and steel. The doctor was wearing an Earth First! t-shirt and drinking a Black Butte Porter, the microbrew of choice for the radical environmental movement. Dr. Murphy knows a lot about treating victims of police brutality and he had prepared a handbook for protesters on how to deal with tear gas, pepper spray, rubber bullets and concussions. Hundreds of copies had been printed and would be passed out to volunteer medics and protesters before the big march on Tuesday.

"Do you think it will come to that?" I asked.

"Well, I hope not," Murphy said. "But if it doesn't, we probably won't have accomplished much, eh?"

Murphy said that the direct action crowd was assembled at a warehouse on East Denny, up toward Seattle Community College. It was a 20-minute walk and I arrived at midnight to a scene of dizzying and cheerful chaos. The Denny Street warehouse was far more than a meeting place; it was part factory, part barracks, part command and control center, part mosh pit. Later on it would become an infirmary.

Inside, so-called affinity groups were planning their separate direct actions; others were constructing giant street puppets, bearing the likeness of corporate titans and politicians, such as Clinton and Maxxam chieftain Charles Hurwitz. Another group, led by Earth First!ers from Eugene, Oregon were putting the finishing touches on what one referred to as the Trojan Horse, a twenty foot-tall, armored siege tower on wheels, capable of holding 14 people. The bulky contraption was designed to be rolled up near the convention center, allowing the people inside to climb out a hatch in the roof and scale over the tops of Metro buses, which the security forces had parked as barricades near the building.

I knew the chief architect of this creation and asked him if he wasn't wasting time and money on such an easy target, as Saddam Hussein had done with his giant, billion dollar cannon destroyed in the first air strike of the Gulf War. "Just wait", he said, a spark of mischief in his eye.

Monday

And the revolution will be started by: sea turtles. At noon about 2,000 people massed at the United Methodist Church, the HQ of the grassroots NGOs, for a march to the convention center. It was environment day and the Earth Island Institute had prepared more than 500 sea turtle costumes for marchers to wear. The sea turtle became the prime symbol of the WTO's threats to environmental laws when a WTO tribunal ruled that the US Endangered Species Act, which requires shrimp to be caught with turtle excluder devices, was an unfair trade barrier.

But the environmentalists weren't the only ones on the street Monday morning. In the first showing of a new solidarity, labor union members from the Steelworkers and the Longshoremen showed up to join the march. In fact, Steelworker Don Kegley led the march, along side environmentalist Ben White. (White was later clubbed in the back of the head by a young man who was apparently angry that he couldn't complete his Christmas shopping. The police pulled the youth away from White, but the man wasn't arrested. White played down the incident.) The throng of sea turtles and blue-jacked union folk took off to the rhythm of a familiar chant that would echo down the streets of Seattle for days: "The people united will never be divided!"

I walked next to Brad Spann, a Longshoreman from Tacoma, who hoisted up one of my favorite signs of the entire week: "Teamsters and Turtles Together At Last!" Brad winked at me and said, "What the hell do you think old Hoffa thinks of that?"

The march, which was too fast and courteous for my taste, was escorted by motorcycle police and ended essentially in a cage, a protest pen next to a construction site near the convention center. A small stage had been erected there hours earlier and Carl Pope, the director of the Sierra Club, was called forth to give the opening speech. The Club is the nation's most venerable environmental group. It's often on the right side of issues, such as old-growth preservation and trade. But in the past decade it has become increasingly a captive of the Democratic Party, and sadly willing to forgive that party's every failing. For example, the Club was adamantly opposed to NAFTA, and helped lead a feisty coalition of green and labor groups in opposition to the treaty. But when Bill Clinton and Al Gore stuffed NAFTA down their throats, there was barely a bleat of protest and the Sierra Club endorsed the free-trade team for a second term in 1996.

I'd never met Carl Pope before and was surprised by what I encountered. He's a tiny man, with a shrill and squeaky voice, who affects the look and hair-flipping mannerisms of RFK circa 1968. Nearing 90, Dave Brower, Pope's more militant predecessor, still has the look of a mountain climber; Pope gives the impression that the only climbing he does is on a StairMaster. I couldn't follow much of what Pope had to say, except that he failed to utter any harsh words about Clinton or Gore, the architects of more than 200 environment-shredding trade deals since 1993. The speech was delivered with a smugness that most of the labor people must have heard as confirmation of their worst fears about the true nature of environmentalists in suits.

Standing near the stage I saw Brent Blackwelder, the head of Friends of the Earth. Behind his glasses and somewhat shambling manner, Blackwelder looks ever so professorial. And he is by far the smartest of the environmental CEOs. But he is also the most radical politically, the most willing to challenge the tired complacency of his fellow green executives. I told him: "Brent, you're the Chomsky of the environmental movement." He chuckled, evidently pleased at the comparison.

Blackwelder was slated to give the next talk and I asked him what he thought of following Carl Pope, a Gore promoter, whose staffers had just plunged a few knives in Blackwelder's back following Friends of the Earth's endorsement of Bill Bradley in the Democratic primaries. He shrugged. "We did our damage." Our endorsement of Bradley stung the Sierra Club almost as much as it did Gore." But Blackwelder wasn't under any illusions about Bradley, either. "Bradley's a free trader. We pleaded with him to at least make a strong statement in opposition to the US position on the timber tariff issue. But he wouldn't budge. There was a real opportunity for him to stick it to Gore and prove himself as the better green."

Blackwelder's speech was a good one, strong and defiant. He excoriated the WTO as a kind of global security force for transnational corporations whose mission is "to stuff unwanted products, like genetically engineered foods, down our throats". Afterwards, I asked Blackwelder what would happen if Clinton announced some environmental sideboard, another meager trust-me pledge. "The plague of Clinton is to say one thing and do another", Blackwelder said. "He talked this line before with NAFTA. But even with the sideboards, everything we said about NAFTA has come true, only worse." I told Blackwelder that I had heard Clinton was going to meet in Seattle on Wednesday with the heads of the National Wildlife, World Wildlife Fund and the Sierra Club. "That's what I hear, too", Blackwelder said. "But he won't meet with us, because he knows we'd call his bluff."

After the speechifying most of the marchers headed back to the church. But a contingent of about 200 ended up in front of McDonald's where a group of French farmers had mustered to denounce US policy on biotech foods. Their leader was Jose Bove, a sheep farmer from Millau in southwest France and a leader of Confederation Paysanne, a French environmental group. In August, Bove had been jailed in France for leading a raid on a McDonald's restaurant under construction in Larzac. At the time, he was already awaiting trial on charges that he destroyed a cache of Novartis' genetically-engineered corn. Bove said his raid on the Larzac McDonald's was prompted by the US's decision to impose a heavy tariff on Roquefort cheese in retaliation for the European Union's refusal to import American hormone-treated beef. Bove's act of defiance earned him the praise of Jacques Chirac and Friends of the Earth. Bove said he was prepared to start a militant worldwide campaign against "Frankenstein" foods. "These actions will only stop when this mad logic comes to a halt", Bove said. "I don't demand clemency but justice."

Bove showed up at the Seattle McDonald's with rounds of Roquefort cheese, which he handed out to the crowd. After listening to a rousing speech against the evils of Monsanto, and its bovine growth hormone and Roundup Ready soybeans, the crowd stormed the McDonald's, breaking its windows and urging the customers and workers to join the marchers on the streets. This was the first shot in the battle for Seattle.

Moments later the block was surrounded by Seattle police, attired in black body armor and Darth Vader-like helmets. Many of them arrived on armored personal carriers, black military trucks referred to affectionately by the TV anchors on the nightly news as "the Peacekeepers". But this time cops held their distance, merely making a show of their firepower and potential to cause havoc. They cordoned off a four block area until the crowd dribbled away in about an hour. At this point, there was a lightness in the air. A big Samoan cop cracked a smile as a protester waved a hunk of stinky cheese in front of his face.

I returned to my hotel early that night. Too exhilarated and exhausted to sleep, I fell back on the bed and flipped on the television. A newscaster was interviewing Michael Moore, the pudgy-faced director of the WTO. "I've always been on the side of the little guy," Moore proclaimed.

Tuesday

Less than 12 hours later, Seattle was under civic emergency, a step away from martial law. National Guard helicopters hovered over downtown, sweeping the city with searchlights. A 7 pm curfew had been imposed and was being flouted by thousands — those same thousands who captured the streets, sustained clouds of tears gas, volleys of rubber bullets, concussion grenades, high powered bean cannons and straightforward beatings with riot batons. The bravery of the street warriors had its tremendous triumph: they held the streets long enough to force the WTO to cancel their opening day. This had been the stated objective of the direct action strategists, and they attained it.

The predicted scenario had been somewhat different. There was to be the great march of organized labor, led by the panjandrums of the AFL-CIO, with James Hoffa Jr. in a starring role. Labor's legions — a predicted 100,000 — were to march from the Space Needle to the Convention Center, clogging the streets and peacefully preventing the WTO delegates from their assembly.

This never happened. The labor chiefs talked tough but accepted a cheap deal. They would get a Wednesday meeting with Bill Clinton, with the promise that at future such WTO conclaves they would get "a seat at the table". So instead of joining the throngs bent on shutting down the opening of the WTO, the big labor rally took place at noon around the Space Needle, some fifteen to twenty blocks from the convention center where the protesters on the front lines were taking their stand. Speaker after speaker took to the podium to address the crowd. None of them mentioned that only blocks away the cops were battering hundreds of demonstrators who were risking their lives to keep the WTO from launching its meetings. When the labor march finally got under way around 1 PM, its marshals directed most of the marchers away from the battle zones down by the convention center. They didn't want to add fuel to the fire or put their members at risk.

For the direct action folks, the morning began in the predawn hours, in a light rain, a thick fog rolling in off Puget Sound. More than 2,000 people massed in Victor Steinbrueck Park, on the waterfront north of Pike's Place market. Once again, steelworkers and Earth First!ers led the way, carrying a banner with the image of a redwood tree and a spotted owl. The march featured giant puppets, hundreds of signs, the ubiquitous sea turtles, singing, chanting, drumming and nervous laughter. There was an atmosphere of carnival to the gathering. New Orleans during Mardi Gras. Juarez on the Day of the Dead. A carnival with an ominous edge.

As the sky finally lightened, I found myself walking next to a group of black men and women trailing a white van. They turned out to be one of the more creative groups in the march, a collection of hip-hop artists from across the country. The van, dubbed the Rap Wagon, carried a powerful sound system capable of rocking the streets, which broadcast a nasty improvised rap called "TKO the WTO". Walking with me up Pine Street to the Roosevelt Hotel was an 18-year old from South Central LA named Thomas. I asked him why he was here. "I like turtles and I hate that fucker Bill Gates", he said. Good enough for me. Thomas and I held hands, forming part of a human chain at the intersection of 7th and Pine, intent on keeping the WTO delegates from reaching their morning meetings.

A British delegate was prevented from entering the convention center after he left the Roosevelt Hotel. He tried to bust through the human chain and was repulsed. Angered, he slugged one of the protesters in the chest and ran down the block towards us. When he reached the corner a small black woman confronted him, shouting: "You hit somebody! I saw you." Whack. The delegate punched the woman in the face, sending her sprawling back into Thomas and me. The scene could have turned ugly, as protesters rushed to protect the woman. But the lead organizer at the corner took control, ushering the crazed delegate into a nearby bookstore.

Meanwhile, a few blocks down the street another frustrated WTO delegate pulled a revolver from his coat pocket and aimed it at protesters blocking the entrance to the Paramount Hotel, where the opening ceremonies were scheduled. The police rushed in with their clubs and jabbed the protesters away from the gun-wielding man, who was neither detained nor stripped of his weapon.

Around 10 am, I ran into my friend Michael Donnelly, a veteran Earth First!er from Oregon. Donnelly and I walked up to 6th and Union, where we heard that a group of forest activists had taken control of an intersection. Here was to come the first violent attack by police on protesters. A band of about 200 protesters had sat down in the street. Others were playing music. Even more were dancing. A squad of riot cops approached. The sergeant mumbled something over a megaphone. "Fifteen minute warning", Donnelly said. "We've got fifteen minutes and then these guys are going to try to clear us out."

About ten minutes later, a Peacekeeper vehicle arrived, more cops clinging to its side. The back of the truck was popped open and dozens of tear gas canisters were unloaded. And, then very suddenly, a tear gas can was launched into the sitting demonstrators. It oozed grey-green smoke. Then seconds later another one. And then five or six more them were fired into the crowd. One of the protesters nearest the cops was a young, petite woman. She rose up, plainly disoriented from the gas, and a Seattle policeman, crouched less than 10 feet away, shot her in the knee with a rubber bullet. She fell to the pavement, grabbing her leg and screaming in pain. Then, moments later, one of her comrades, maddened by the unprovoked attack, charged the police line, Kamikaze-style. Two cops beat him to the ground with their batons, hitting him at least 20 times. As the cops flailed away with their four-foot long clubs, the crowd chanted, "The whole world is watching, the whole world is watching". Soon the man started to rise. Somehow he got on his hands and knees and then he was shot in the back by a cop who was standing over him. His hands were cuffed behind him and he was dragged away across the pavement.

The so-called rubber bullets are meant to be fired at areas of the body with large muscle mass. Like the thighs or the ass. But over the next two days Seattle cops would fire off thousands of rounds without exhibiting any caution. Dozens of people, none of them threatening the cops with harm, were shot in the back, in the neck, in the groin, in the face; in places that the ammunition's manufacturers, ever conscious of liability questions, warn could cause severe trauma or death.

By now another volley of tear gas had been throw into the

crowd and the intersection was clotted with fumes. At first I was stunned, staring at the scene with the glazed look of the freshly lobotomized. Then my eyes began to boil in my head, my lips burned and it seemed impossible to draw a breath. When it's raining, the chemical agents hug close to the ground, taking longer to dissolve into the air. This compounds the tear gas' stinging power, its immobilizing effect. I staggered back up 6th Avenue toward University, where I stumbled into a cop decked out in his storm trooper gear. He turned and gave me a swift whack to my side with the tip of his riot club. I feel to my knees and covered my head, fearing a tumult of blows. But the blows never came and soon I felt a gentle hand on my shoulder and woman's voice say, "Come here".

I retreated into a narrow alley and saw the blurry outline of a young woman wearing a Stetson cowboy hat and a gas mask. "Lean your head back, so that I can wash the chemicals out of your eyes", she said. The water was cool and within seconds I could see again. "Who are you?" I asked. "Osprey", she said, and disappeared into the chemical mist. Osprey, the familiar, totemic name of an Earth First!er. Thank god for Edward Abbey.

But the battle going on at 6th and University was far from over. The police moved in on a group of protesters from Humboldt County, northern California, who had locked themselves together with cement casts on their arms, thus immobilizing themselves in the middle of the intersection. They were ordered to evacuate the area, which of course they couldn't and wouldn't do. Then after this obligatory warning the cops attacked ferociously, dousing them in the face with spurts of pepper spray and then dropping searing tear gas canisters on top of them. After a few minutes, the valiant police fell upon the helpless protesters with their batons. Two of the dozen or so protesters were knocked unconscious, the rest were bloodied and bruised. But the group held its ground for hours and by 2 pm the cops had backed off. The University intersection had been held.

Pepper spray (oleoresin capsicum) has a nasty history. But it is becoming more and more popular with police departments as part of their arsenal of "safe" weapons. Pepper spray is often used in situations where cops could otherwise handle the situation without violence. In Seattle the cops were using a 10 percent solution, carted around in containers that looked link mini-fire extinguishers. Pepper spray this potent has been linked to more than 100 fatalities in the US and Canada, often from allergic reactions or suffocation of the victim after being sprayed, tackled and cuffed. Despite this, law enforcement agencies have done almost no scientific studies on the effects of the toxin on human health. And there's no federal or state agency that regulates the manufacture or use of the chemical.

The Seattle cops used MK-46 First Defense Red Pepper manufactured by Defense Technologies (Def-Tech) in Caspar, Wyoming. Pepper spray is made from extracts of capsicum peppers mixed with an alcohol solution that causes intense burning of the skin, nose, mouth and eyes. Def-Tech cautions that the toxin is meant only to used for defensive purposes, to protect the safety of a cop and shouldn't be sprayed on people at a distance of less than three feet. This warning was routinely flouted by the Seattle police who liberally sprayed the stinging solution directly into the face and even on the genitals of demonstrators.

Who were these direct action warriors on the front lines? Earth First, the Alliance for Sustainable Jobs and the Environment (the new enviro-steelworker alliance), the Ruckus Society (a direct action training center), Jobs with Justice, Rainforest Action Network, Food Not Bombs, Global Exchange and a small contingent of Anarchists, the dreaded Black Bloc.

There was also a robust international contingent on the streets Tuesday morning: French farmers, Korean greens, Canadian wheat growers, Mexican environmentalists, Chinese dissidents, Ecuadorian anti-dam organizers, U'wa tribespeople from the Colombian rainforest and British campaigners against genetically modified foods. Indeed earlier, a group of Brits had cornered two Monsanto lobbyists behind an abandoned truck carrying an ad for the Financial Times. They detained the corporate flacks long enough to deliver a stern warning about the threat of frankencrops to wildlife, such as the Monarch butterfly. Then a wave of tear gas wafted over them and the Monsanto men fled, covering their eyes with their neckties.

By noon, around the convention center, the situation was desperate. The Seattle police, initially comparatively restrained, were now losing control. They were soon supplemented by the Kings County sheriffs' department, a rough mob, who seemed to get their kicks from throwing concussion grenades into crowds, with the M-80-like devices often exploding only inches above the heads of people.

Around 12:30 someone smashed the first storefront window. It could have been an anarchist. It could have been an agent provocateur or a stray bullet or concussion grenade. What's clear, though, is that the vandalism — what there was of it — started more than two hours after the cops had attacked nonviolent protesters amassed at 6th and Union. Protesters who had offered themselves up for arrest. At most, the dreaded Black Bloc, which was to become demonized by the press and some of the more staid leaders of labor and green groups, amounted to 50 people, many of them young women. Much of the so-called looting that took place was done not by the Anarchists, but by Seattle street gangs.

As the day ticked away the street protesters kept asking, "Where are the labor marchers?" Many expected that at any moment thousands of longshoremen and Teamsters would reinforce them in the fray. Those absent labor legions never came. The marshals for the union march steered the big crowds away from the action. The isolation of the street protesters allowed the cops to get far more violent.

Even in the run-up to WTO week in Seattle, the genteel element — foundation careerists, NGO bureaucrats, policy wonks — was raising cautionary fingers, saying that the one thing to be avoided in Seattle this week was civil disobedience. The internet was thick with tremulous admonitions about the need for good behavior, the perils of playing into the enemies' hands, the profound necessity for decorous — i.e., passive — comportment. Their fondest hope was to attend, in mildly critical posture, not only the WTO conclave in Seattle, but all future ones. This too became the posture of big labor. On Tuesday, in answer to a question from CNN's Bernard Shaw on whether labor wanted to kill the WTO, James Hoffa Jr. replied, "No. We want to get labor a seat at the table".

Eventually, several phalanxes of union marchers skirted their herders and headed up 4th Avenue to the battlegrounds at Pine and Pike. Most of them seemed to be from the more militant unions, the Steelworkers, IBEW and the Longshoremen. And they seemed to be pissed at the political penury of their leaders. Randal McCarthy, a Longshoreman from Kelso, Washington, told me: "That fucker, Sweeney. No wonder we keep getting rolled. If he were any dumber, he'd be in management."

For a couple hours there had been an eerie lull in the tear gas assaults. Out on the streets no one knew that the cops had run out of gas and had had to send a supply plane to Montana, where they picked up 3,300 pounds of more toxic CN gas, known to chemists as 1-choloracetophenol and to police bureaucrats as a "less lethal" munition. Less lethal indeed.

Now reloaded the cops went on a rampage. A report by the Washington chapter of the American Civil Liberties Union crisply summed up the sadistic behavior of the cops that afternoon: "Officers struck or pepper sprayed people who posed no physical threat, were not resisting arrest, or were not being allowed to leave the scene. Some officers singled out people who questioned police authority or said things uncomplimentary to the police, and bystanders who were simply walking down the street."

At 3:24 pm the mayor of Seattle, egged on by a furious Madeleine Albright, who had spent the morning boiling in rage over being locked down in her hotel, declared a civic emergency, the equivalent of martial law in the heart of America's most self-consciously liberal city. A rigid curfew was imposed. People were to be off the streets from 7pm to 7am. One immediate effect was to give the cops, whose ranks were now swollen with raw recruits from across the state of Washington, a greenlight to bully and bash their way across the streets of downtown. By 4pm, Seattle had become a free-fire zone for cops and nearly everyone, protesters, workers, shoppers and even other cops, were targets. A few hours later the city banned the sale, purchase and possession of gas masks. The initial order was so sweeping that it later had to be amended to exempt police and military personnel.

These emergency orders and closures came rapidly It's stunning to experience how quickly a city can be turned into a police state. The decisions were made by executive fiat from the mayor. Ultimately, the Seattle City council ratified all the repressive measures —- but not until December 6, a week after the initial declaration of a civic emergency.

By darkness on Tuesday the 2,000 or so street warriors had won the day, even though they were finally forced to retreat north and east out of the city center and into the neighborhood of Capitol Hill. The opening ceremonies for the WTO ministerial had been cancelled. But suppose 30,000 union people had reinforced them? Downtown could have been held all night, and the convention center sealed off. Maybe even President Clinton would have been forced to stay away.

And what about that siege tower? Well, it turned out to be an excellent diversionary tactic. When the Seattle police's SWAT teams converged to disable the Earth First!ers strange contraption, it gave the direct action groups time to secure their positions, successfully encircling the convention center, the nearby hotels and WTO venues. In an odd way it may have been a key to the great victory of the day.

Wednesday

Wednesday was the turning point of the week. After the crackdown of Tuesday night, where even Christmas carollers in a residential area were gassed, many wondered who would show up to confront the WTO, Bill Clinton, the police and the national guard the next morning. More than a thousand, it turned out. And the numbers grew as the day wore on. The resistance had proved its resilience.

Our presence in downtown was no longer wanted. In fact, it was illegal. The mayor had ordered 25 square blocks of downtown cordoned off. The heart of the city was a "no protest zone" with entry controlled by the police. The mayor made a few exceptions: Seattle was open to WTO delegates; business owners and workers; downtown residents; security and emergency personnel and, tellingly, holiday shoppers. The closure itself was a stark violation of the US constitution and a US Supreme Court case called Collins v. Jordan, which compels municipal governments to permit protests close enough so that they can be heard and seen by the intended audience.

But the Seattle officials, under the goads of the Clinton security team, went further. Their goal was to suppress, not riots or looting or even civil disobedience, but political speech. The cops were told to bar any visible signs of protest against the WTO or dissent against police tactics, including signs, leaflets, buttons and even t-shirts. This situation soon became dangerously absurd. About 10 am on Wednesday a gang of cops body-slammed a protester who was standing on 6th Avenue handing out leaflets. The text was far from incendiary. It was merely a copy of a New York Times story from that morning on the cops' rampages of the day before. Another squad of censors with guns detained a man who was handing out to passersby on the sidewalk sheets of paper containing the text of the Bill of Rights. His stash of papers was confiscated.

The morning's first march headed down Denny Street from Seattle Community College toward downtown. The 250 marchers were met at about 7am by a line of cops in riot gear at 6th Avenue. A sobering sign that things had become more serious was the sight of cops armed with AR-15 assault rifles. Some brave soul went up to one of the deputies and asked, "Do those shoot rubber bullets?" "Nope", the cop replied through a Darth Vader-like microphone embedded in his gas mask. "This is the real thing." Dozen of protesters were arrested immediately, placed in plastic wrist cuffs and left sitting on the street for hours—more than were arrested all day on Tuesday.

Watching all this were attorneys from National Lawyer's Guild. The NLG had sent dozens of legal observers to Seattle to record incidents of police brutality and to advise demonstrators on how to act after being arrested. On Denny Street that morning I met Marge Buckley, a lawyer from Los Angeles. She was wearing a green t-shirt with "NLG Legal Observer" printed across the front and was furiously writing notes on a pad. Buckley said she had filled several notepads on Tuesday with tales of unwarranted and unprovoked shootings, gassings and beatings.

"Look!" Buckley said, as we trotted down the sidewalk to catch up with the marchers who had abandoned Denny Street, seeking another entry point into city center. "How weird. The people are obeying traffic signals on their way to a civil disobedience action." A few moments later I lost track of Buckley, when the police, including a group mounted on horses, encircled the marchers at Rainier Square. I slipped through the line just as the Seattle police sergeant yelled, "Gas!" Someone later said she had been arrested.

I wouldn't be surprised if Buckley had been nabbed. The

police had begun targeting the "command-and-control" of the demonstrators — people with cellphones, bullhorns, the known faces and suspected organizers, medics and legal observers.

The NLG folks were near the top of the list. At 7:56 on Wednesday morning, over the following message went out over police radios to Seattle street cops: "Heads up! FYI! We are having some legal observers probing our lines, taking notes on our posts. So if any officer around the Convention Center sees these folks, wearing green, legal observers—they're taking notes. Take the notes from them and get 'em outta here."

Several of the plainclothes cops at the Denny Street encounter had photos in their hands and were scanning them to identify the lead organizers. As the marchers occupied the intersection singing "We Shall Overcome", about 20 police formed into a wedge and quickly attacked the protesters, seized a bald-headed man talking on a cellphone (it seemed nearly everyone in Seattle had a cellphone and a camera) and dragged him back to the police line. The man was John Sellers, director of the Ruckus Society. Sellers was held for an hour, then released.

Later the police hierarchy grappled for excuses, even claiming that they had been taken outmaneuvered by the protesters' "sophisticated use of cellphones and walkie talkies."

On Wednesday afternoon, I encountered Kirk Murphy, the doctor. His Earth First! t-shirt had been replaced by a business suit and a rain jacket. I raised my eyebrows at him. He said, "I'm trying hard not to look like part of the support team. They've arrested a lot of our medics and I need to stay out of jail to help the injured."

These targeted arrests may have been meant to turn the protests into the chaotic mess the city's pr people were stigmatizing to the media. But it didn't happen. The various groups of protesters, sometimes in the hundreds, huddled together and decided their next course of action by a rudimentary form of consensus. Everyone was given a chance to have a say, then a vote was taken on what to do next and, usually, the will of the majority was followed without significant disruptions. The problem was that it slowed down the marches, allowing the police and National Guard troops to box in the protesters, most tragically later Wednesday evening at Pike's Place Market.

As the march turned up toward the Sheraton and was beaten back by cops on horses, I teamed up with Etienne Vernet and Ronnie Cumming. Cumming is the head of one of the feistiest groups in the US, the PureFood Campaign, Monsanto's chief pain in the ass. Cumming hails from the oil town of Port Arthur, Texas. He went to Cambridge with another great foe of industrial agriculture, Prince Charles. Cumming was a civil rights organizer in Houston during the mid-sixties. "The energy here is incredible," Cumming said. "Black and white, labor and green, Americans, Europeans, Africans and Asians arm-in-arm. It's the most hopeful I've felt since the height of the civil rights movement."

Vernet lives in Paris, where he is a leader of the radical

green group EcoRopa. At that very moment the European Union delegates inside the convention were capitulating on a key issue: the EU, which had banned import of genetically engineered crops and hormone-treated beef, had agreed to a US proposal to establish an scientific committee to evaluate the health and environmental risks of biotech foods, a sure first step toward undermining the moratorium. Still Vernet was in a jolly mood, lively and invigorated, if a little bemused by the decorous nature of the crowd. "Americans seem to have been out of practice in these things", he told me. "Everyone's so polite. The only things on fire are dumpsters filled with refuse." He pointed to a shiny black Lexus parked on Pine Street, which the throngs of protesters had scrupulously avoided. In the windshield was a placard identifying it as belonging to a WTO delegate. "In Paris that car would be burning."

Somehow Etienne and I made it through four police barricades all the way across town to the International Media Center, a briefing area hosted by Public Citizen in the Seattle Center, a cramped Greek Revival-style structure. I was there to interview my old friend, Dave Brower and Steelworker David Foster. The two Daves were late and to pass time I sat down in front of a TV. There was Bill Clinton speaking at the Port of Seattle. His verbal sleight-of-hand routine was masterful. He denounced Tuesday's violence, but said the WTO delegates should listen to the "legitimate" protesters. He said he disagreed with most of their views, but suggested that some should at least be permitted to observe the proceedings. Later that day

Clinton met with the obeisant green leaders, including National Wildlife's Mark van Puten, the Sierra Club's Carl Pope and World Resources Institute chairman William Ruckleshaus. Ruckleshaus is also a longtime board member of Weyerhaeuser, the Seattle-based transnational timber company. On Thursday, environmentalists held a large demonstration outside the downtown offices of the timber company's realty wing. Needless to say, the leaders of the big green groups didn't show up for that one.

Clinton talked about having the WTO incorporate environmental sidebars into its rulemaking. But then the administration didn't back away from its Global Logging Amendment, an accelerated reduction in tariffs on the global timber trade. George Frampton, head of the Council on Environmental Quality and former head of the Wilderness Society, appeared at a press conference later in the day and stiff-armed the greens. "Knowledgeable environmentalists shouldn't have anything against the measure", Frampton said. His voice reeked with condescension. In fact, this was the one issue on which all the big groups were united in opposition to the US position.

"This follows the tried and true Clinton formula: kiss 'em, then fuck 'em over", said Steve Spahr, a bus driver, computer repairman and ancient forest defender from Salem, Oregon.

Clinton called the events outside his suite in the Westin "a rather interesting hoopla." The president expressed sympathy for the views of those in the streets at the very moment his aides were ordering Seattle Mayor Paul Shell (aka "Mayor Shellshocked") to use all available force to clear the streets. There is now no question but that the most violent attacks by the police and the National Guard came at the instigation of the White House and not the mayor or the police chief. And, in fact, CNN reported that the Clinton administration has once again violated the Posse Comitatus Act by sending in a contingent from the US military to the scene. More than 160 members of the Domestic Military Support Force were sent to Seattle on Tuesday, including troops from the Special Forces division and the Delta Force. Clinton, of course, was later quite happy to blame Mayor Schell, the Seattle police, and the WTO, itself, for both the chaos and the crackdown, while offering himself as a peacemaker to the very battle he provoked.

While Clinton was jabbering on, Victor Menotti became the latest victim of police brutality. Menotti is an environmental trade specialist for the International Forum on Globalization, an acrid critic of the WTO, also a policy wonk and a good one. He was a credentialed WTO observer. Menotti had been attending a briefing by Clinton administration reps and other WTO officials on a global logging initiative. The meeting had taken a bad turn. Menotti, carrying a sheaf of papers, took a break from the dismal session inside the convention center and went outside to brief his colleagues on the street. "It looks like your worst fears have been realized", Menotti said. In other words, the Clinton administration had once again caved into the pressures of the multinational timber giants. Then there was a sudden flurry of activity, at the nearby corner of 5th and Pike. "I saw the crowd in front of me reel back and turn and run, and I just looked over my shoulder and saw black ponchos flying and the sticks in the air, and I just fled myself", Menotti said. He recalls scooting down the street for about a block. He negotiated his way around a parked car and then it dawned on him that the police were after him for some reason. "I just thought, `There's no reason to run", Menotti said. He was arrested, his papers seized and he was hauled off to jail. "I kept thinking: who was it that targeted me for arrest."

The police report says Menotti was arrest for "obstructing an officer." But he was never charged. Even so, he spent the night in the King County Jail. It was in that jail cell that Menotti met Gezai Yihdego, a 35-year old black Seattlite who had been born in war-torn Etitrea. It immediately struck Menotti that Yihdego didn't look like the typical WTO protester. He wasn't. Yihdego was a cab driver. On Wednesday morning he was cruising past the Madison hotel when he was flagged down by a woman. He picked her up and pulled back into traffic, but was almost immediately thereafter halted by a policeman. The cop reached into Yihdego's window and sharply pulled the steering wheel to the left.

"'Sir, I have a passenger', Yihdego told the cop. 'And you may put our lives in danger. Don't pull this. It's my car. You have no right to touch my car, my property.' But he opened the door and tried to push me hard to the right. I resisted that and I said, 'This is my car. Get out.' Then he started to drag me out.'"

Yihdego's frightened passenger wasn't an ordinary citizen, but a member of the Clinton administration and an official WTO delegate. She later told the Seattle Times that she had objected to the treatment of Yihdego, but she was still so frightened that she wanted to remain nameless. "The policeman opened the door, grabbed the cab driver, threw him to the ground, and there were six other officers that surrounded him," she said. "I'm just stunned."

The Clinton administration official told the cops that the cab driver had done nothing wrong and that they should leave him alone. They didn't. One of the cops jerked Yihdego up off the pavement and shouted, "Where are you from?"

"Hell, look, man, what does that have to do with anything?" Yihdego said. "Are you arresting me for being foreign? For having an accent? For being black? For being a taxi driver?"

Over the protest of the Clinton administration official, Yihdego was carted off to jail. Neither he nor Menotti were ever charged with a crime.

Eventually, Clinton shut up and Brower and Foster walked into the room. Brower was breaking new ground once again by pulling together a new group of trade unionists and greens. At 87 years old, Brower, the arch druid, is finally beginning to show his age. He walks with a cane. A pacemaker regulates his heartbeat. He is fighting bladder cancer. And he can't drink as many dry martinis as he used to. But his mind is still as agile as an antelope, his intellectual vision startlingly clear and radical.

"Today, the police in Seattle have proved they are the handmaidens of the corporations"' Brower said. "But something else has been proved. And that's that people are starting to stand up and say: we won't be transnational victims."

Brower was joined by David Foster, director for District 11 of the United Steelworkers of America, one of the most articulate and unflinching labor leaders in America. Earlier this year, Brower and Foster formed an unlikely union, a coalition of radical environmentalists and Steelworkers called the Alliance for Sustainable Jobs and the Environment, which had just run an amusing ad in the New York Times asking "Have You Heard the One About the Environmentalist and the Steelworker". The groups had found they had a common enemy: Charles Hurwitz, the corporate raider. Hurwitz owned the Pacific Lumber Company, the northern California timber firm that is slaughtering some of the last stands of ancient redwoods on the planet. At the same time, Hurwitz, who also controlled Kaiser Aluminum, had locked out 3,000 Steelworkers at Kaiser's factories in Washington, Ohio and Louisiana. "The companies that attack the environment most mercilessly are often also the ones that are the most anti-union," Foster told me. "More unites us than divides us."

I came away thinking that for all its promise this tenuous marriage might end badly. Brower, the master of ceremonies, isn't going to be around forever to heal the wounds and cover up the divisions. There are deep, inescapable issues that will, inevitably, pit Steelworkers, fighting for their jobs in an ever-tightening economy, against greens, defending dwindling species like sockeye salmon that are being killed off by the hydrodams that power the aluminum plants that offer employment to steel workers. When asked about this potential both Brower and Foster danced around it skillfully. But it was a dance of denial. The tensions won't go away simply because the parties agree not to mention them in public. Indeed, they might even build, like a pressure cooker left unwatched. I shook the thought from my head. For this moment, the new, powerful solidarity was too seductive to let such broodings intrude for long.

If anything could anneal the alliance together it was the actions of the Seattle cops and National Guard, who, until Wednesday afternoon, had displayed a remarkable reluctance to crackdown on unionists. The Steelworkers had gotten permission from the mayor for a sanctioned march from the Labor Temple to the docks, where they performed a mock "Seattle Steel Party", dumping styrofoam steel girders into the waters of Elliot Bay which, showing their new-found green conscience, they fished back out.

When the rally broke up, hundreds of Steelworkers joined with other protesters in an impromptu march down 1st Avenue. As the crowd reached Pike Place Market, they found paramilitary riot squads waiting for them and were rocked with fusillades of military-strength CN gas, flash bombs, and larger rubber bullets, about a half-inch in diameter. The carnage was indiscriminate. Holiday shoppers and Metro buses were gassed. In an effort to jack up the intimidation, the cop squads were marching in goose-stepping fashion, smacking their riot clubs against their shin-guards to create a sinister sound with echoes back to Munich. This was the most violent of the street battles that I witnessed, involving hundreds of police and more than 20 tear gas attacks.

Repeated volleys of concussion grenades were launched over the crowd, sending many people diving down onto the pavement and others scurrying into storefronts for safety. After one tremendous explosion a Seattle cop was caught on the department's videotape exclaiming, "That was sweet!"

There is a certain species of pacifist who finds any outward expression of outrage embarrassing. Thus it was that demonstrators at nearly every corner and barricade were being cautioned "not to retaliate" against police attacks. They were even warned not to throw the tear gas cans back toward the police lines. But, of course, that was the safest place for them. They weren't going to hurt the cops, who were decked out in the latest chemical warfare gear.

That night at Pike Place Market a can of tear gas landed at my feet. Next to me were a young woman and her four-year-old son. As the woman pulled her child inside her raincoat to protect him from the poison gas, I reached down, grabbed the canister and heaved it back toward the advancing black wall of cops. The can was so hot it seared my hand. Expecting to be shot at, I dove behind the nearest dumpster and saw a familiar face. It was

Thomas, one of the rappers I'd walked with on Tuesday morning. We huddled close together, shielding our eyes from the smoke and gas. "Now all these muthafuckas up here have a taste of what it's like in Compton nearly every night", Thomas screamed.

When the cops are on the streets in force, black people always pay the price. As Thomas and I were ducking flash bombs and rubber bullets, Seattle police were busy harassing Richard McIver, a black Seattle City Councilman who was on his way to a WTO reception at the Westin Hotel. Even though McIver flashed the police with his embossed gold business card identifying him as a councilman, the police denied him entry. They pulled him roughly from his car and threatened to place him in handcuffs. Rep. Dennis Kucinich, the Democrat from Ohio, witnessed this scene. "I'm 58 years old," McIver said. "I had on a $400 suit, but last night I was just another nigger."

Seattle had become a proving ground for what defense theorists have dubbed "asymmetrical warfare", urban assaults against a city's own citizens. The Seattle officials claimed they were caught off guard, hamstrung by a city ordinance that prevented them from doing covert investigations. But the organizing for the Seattle protests weren't much of a secret. What hadn't already been reported by the New York Times and Wall Street Journal was available for the cops to study on numerous web sites. Even the irascible Ruckus Society attempted to negotiate mass arrests with the police. But the deputy chief told John Sellers that they simply didn't have the manpower to handle it in such a coordinated fashion. Sellers smiled and replied, "We can live with that".

The moaning from the cops was a weak attempt to cover their ass and to strike at a hated restriction on their police powers, the Seattle Police Investigations Ordinance. The measure prohibits Seattle police from infiltrating and spying on individuals and groups for reasons based solely on their political affiliations and opinions, an entirely sensible law that was passed in 1979 after it came to light that Seattle police had amassed thousands of dossiers on people and groups because of their politics, not any evidence of wrongdoing.

Seattle police said they responded aggressively only when their officers were hit with rocks, bottles, Molotov cocktails. Well, frankly, this is bullshit. Seattle isn't Beirut. There's no rocky rubble on the streets of the Emerald City. In fact, there weren't any glass bottles, either. In the eight or nine confrontations I witnessed, the most the cops were hit with were some half-full plastic water bottles and a few lightweight sticks that had been used to hold cardboard signs.

Despite the fear-mongering by the police and Clinton administration flacks, the evidence of a civilian riot was non-existent. With tens of thousands of demonstrators on the streets for a week, under near constant assault by cops, there were no firearms confiscated, no Molotov cocktails discovered and no police officers seriously injured —— though many later claimed disabilities for stress, anxiety, and exhaustion. Most of the 56 officers who filled out injury reports were victims of friendly fire—hit by concussion grenades, overcome from tear gas and pepper spray, suffered burns from mishandling tear gas canisters, hearing-loss from grenades and gunfire. One officer even claimed that a tight-fitting gas mask cracked several of his teeth.

In the end, what was vandalized? Mainly the boutiques of Sweatshop Row: Nordstrom's, Adidas, the Gap, Bank of America, Niketown, Old Navy, Banana Republic and Starbucks. The expressions of destructive outrage weren't anarchic, but extremely well-targeted. The manager of Starbucks whined about how "mindless vandals" destroyed his window and tossed bags of French Roast onto the street. But the vandals weren't mindless. They didn't bother the independent streetside coffee shop across the way. Instead, they lined up and bought cup after cup. No good riot in Seattle could proceed without a shot of espresso.

These minor acts of retribution served as a kind of Gulf of Tonkin incident. They were used to justify the violent onslaughts by the police and the National Guard. Predictably, the leaders of the NGOs were fast to condemn the protesters. The World Trade Observer is a daily tabloid produced during the convention by the mainstream environmental groups and the Nader shop. Its Wednesday morning edition contained a stern denunciation of the direct action protests that had shut down the WTO the day before. The Sierra Club's Carl Pope repudiated the violence of the protests, saying it delegitimized the position of the NGOs. He did not see fit to criticize the actions of the police.

But even Pope was outdone by Medea Benjamin, the diminutive head of Global Exchange, who had sent her troops out to protect the facades of Niketown and the Gap from being defaced by protesters. Benjamin was quoted in the New York Times as saying: "Here we are protecting Nike, McDonald's, The Gap, and all the while I'm thinking, 'Where are the police? These anarchists should have been arrested.' " Of course, Nike is used to police intervening to protect its factories from worker actions in places like Indonesia and Vietnam and it's depressing to see Benjamin calling for such crackdowns in Seattle.

The assault on Niketown didn't begin with the anarchists, but with protesters who wanted to get a better view of the action. They got the idea from Rainforest Action Network activists who had free-climbed the side of a building across the street and unfurled a huge banner depicting a rattlesnake, coiled and ready to strike, with the slogan, "Don't Trade on Me".

Occupying the intersection in front of Niketown guarded by Benjamin and her Global Exchange troops was a group of Korean farmers and greens, several were dressed in their multicolored traditional garb. It's no secret why they picked this corner. For decades, Nike has exploited Korean workers in its Asian sweatshops. These folks cheered wildly and banged their copper kettles when a climber scaled the façade of Nike's storefront, stripped the chrome letters off the Niketown sign and tossed them to the crowd, as Nike store managers in the window a floor above grazed on garden burgers. The action should have warmed the hearts of nearly everyone, even the

Seattle Downtown Beautification Association. For one brief moment, the city of Seattle had been rid of an architectural blight. As Harper's magazine reported a few years ago the black-and-silver neo-noir stylings of Niketown outlets bear an eerie resemblance to the designs concocted by Albert Speer for the Third Reich.

The cops finally overreached that night when they backed us up into the Capitol Hill district, the densest residential neighborhood north of San Francisco. The area was far outside the curfew zone and the cop-designated no protest area. But more than a hundred cops came anyway, ludicrously claiming that the protesters might take over the East Precinct building.

Brian Derdowski had a different recollection. Derdowski is a member of the King County council. When he saw the tv coverage of the cops driving the protesters up into the Capitol Hill district, he went there himself. For the next four hours he tried to mediate between the cops and the protesters and residents. But he was gassed himself and took down accounts of police driving vans directly into the crowd. "The police were going around in vans, approaching groups of demonstrators and residents, jumping out of vehicles, using tear gas and rubber bullets on people, then jumping back into the vehicles and driving away", Derdowski recalled.

People watching tv late that night saw a cop accost a man on the sidewalk, poke him in the chest with his baton, kick him in the groin and then, for good measure, shoot him in the neck with a rubber bullet. The man wasn't a WTO protester, but a resident who had been gassed out of his home.

Another strange story from that night was recorded by a National Lawyer's Guild attorney from a worker trapped in his downtown office building on Wednesday afternoon: "The witness states that he left his downtown work at 3:30 that day. Aware of what had been going on, he states he asked an officer if it was safe to leave. The officer reportedly stated that it was a peaceful protest and no tear gas would be fired. The worker states he had walked a few blocks and was hit with CS gas. As he turned to leave, he was disoriented by concussive grenades, and hit again with gas. He then returned to his place of work and disposed of his ruined contact lenses. He tried to leave again at 5 pm, but was gassed. Later that evening, he returned to his home at Capitol Hill. Here he witnessed police shooting rubber bullets and tear gas at residents and into a business. Standing near his house he was shot with rubber bullets."

Around midnight a woman got off work at a restaurant in Capitol Hill. Her boyfriend had come to escort her home through the battle-strewn streets. She later told her story to ACLU investigators: "An officer said, 'Get the fuck out of here'. Then he hit my boyfriend with his nightstick. My boyfriend said, 'We are not protesters, we are just walking home'. And the officer hit him again. By then there was another officer and they pushed us up against the storefront and frisked us. An officer said, 'You've no idea what we've been through today'. They then sprayed my friend with pepper spray and handcuffed him. As they hauled him off to the squad car, I started back to the restaurant to get my boss. When I turned back to look at him again, an officer sprayed me in the face with pepper spray."

It was a little after 2 am. There were less than a hundred of us left on the street. We faced even more cops. Someone began to sing Silent Night. And the final assault of gas and grenades was launched. I stumbled back to the King's Inn and finally got to sleep with the words of John Goodman, a locked-out steelworker from Spokane, ringing in my head. "The things I've seen here in Seattle I never thought I'd see America."

Thursday

The next morning I was coughing up small amounts of blood, 600 demonstrators were in jail, the police were on the defensive over their tactics and the WTO conference itself was coming apart at the seams.

Those under arrest had been hauled off to the old Sand Point naval base, where many of them sat for hours in crowded busses. In most cases, the arresting officers didn't write individual arrest reports. Many of the arrestees were offered a deal: they would be released on the condition that they not re-enter the downtown area. It was a deal few took. They were essentially tortured for their refusal. Most were held for more than 72-hours without being arraigned, allowed medical attention or contact with their attorneys.

And some were savagely beaten. There were more than 300 reports of brutality against protesters inside Seattle's jails.

In the end there were 631 arrests, all but 24 on misdemeanor charges such as obstructing pedestrian traffic or failure to disperse. The charges against 511 of the arrestees were dismissed. Only 14 cases actually went to trial and there the Seattle DA's record was far from impressive: 10 plea bargains, 2 guilty verdicts and 2 acquittals.

Inside the WTO, the Africa nations had shown the same solidarity as the protesters on the streets. They refused to buckle to US demands and drew from US Trade Rep. Charlene Barshevsky a blunt threat: "I reiterated to the ministers that if we are unable to achieve that goal I fully reserve the right to also use an exclusive process to achieve a final outcome. There's no question about my right as a chair to do it or my intention to do it, but it is not the way I want this to be done." Despite the heavy-handed bluster, the African delegates hung together and the WTO talks collapsed.

I walked out on the street one last time. The acrid stench of CN gas still soured the morning air. As I turned to get into my car for the drive back to Portland, a black teenager grabbed my arm. "Hey, man, does this WTO deal come to town every year?" I knew how the kid felt. Along with the poison, the flash bombs and rubber bullets, there was an optimism, energy and camaraderie that I hadn't felt in a long time

Chapter 3

Who Won? What Was The Victory?

Hardly had the tear gas dispersed from the streets of downtown Seattle before an acrid struggle broke out over the nature of the protests and their objectives, as well as who should claim the spoils. The fighting — often piously denounced as "mere backbiting" or fostering hated "disunity" — was vital, inasmuch as it helped clarify what the proper aims of a radical attack on the WTO should be.

The pro WTO, "free market" chorus, (in which almost all corporate journalists are to be counted), was predictable in the venom of its slurs on those who fought the police in the streets, even those who marched in orderly fashion in Big Labor's rally. Thomas Friedman of the New York Times furiously stigmatized "these anti-WTO protesters—who are a Noah's ark of flat-earth advocates, protectionist trade unions and yuppies looking for their 1960s fix." Friedman is a columnist of awesome vulgarity in both tone and content, who distills the pretensions of "the new globalism" at their most brashly strident. "Blow up a different power station in Iraq every day", his Times column urged in January, 1999. He made the same advocacy of a war crime three months later, urging the terror bombing of Yugoslavia: "It should be lights out in Belgrade: every power grid, water pipe, bridge, road…"

Friedman exhibits on a weekly basis one of the severest cases known to science of Lippmann's Condition, named for the legendary journalistic hot-air salesman, Walter Lippmann, and alluding to the inherent tendency of these quasi-official government spokesmen to swell in self-importance to zeppelin-like dimensions. Friedman's conceit is legendary. "I have won not one, but two Pulitzer prizes, and I won't stand for being called a liar by the next president, " George Stephanopoulos recalls (in his memoir All Too Human) Friedman shouting down the phone during the Clinton transition in early 1993.

Friedman is never happier than when foraging in corporate suites. His book The Lexus and The Olive Tree is an extended paean to the US-based corporate dominion over the planet. Open it to almost any page and one finds something like this: "In October 1995, I flew out to Redmond, Washington, to interview Microsoft's number-two man, president Steve Ballmer, in order to ask him one simple question." (So why didn't he e-mail him?)

The use of the first person pronoun in Friedman's work is profuse (e.g., 20 uses of the first person singular in the course of one 34-line paragraph starting on page 20 of the paperback reissue of The Lexus and the Olive Tree). This endlessly intrusive I is permanently locked in an elevator at a Davos Summit in perpetual session of the world's Important People, to whom he pays fervent tribute. Like most journalists who spend their time in the corporate elevator, Friedman is an assiduous bootlicker. Take his citations of the Monsanto chairman, Robert

Shapiro. Page 87: "Robert Shapiro...is a classic example of a chief executive who revamped the center of his company so the buck could start, not stop there." Page 182: "Robert Shapiro... once remarked to me that his company is not on a crusade for spreading anticorrupt practices. But not paying bribes is how it does its own business, and he is keenly aware that in so doing Monsanto is helping to seed the world with people who share its values." Page 226: "Robert Shapiro... likes to say that there are always a few things that it pays to keep secret..." Page 281: "As Robert Shapiro of Monsanto likes to say: 'Human population multiplied by human aspirations for a middle-class existence divided by the current technological tool kit is putting unsustainable strains on the biological systems that support life on our planet...'"

Yes, this is Robert Shapiro, the world-class asshole who took a company making billions out of the herbicide Roundup and who almost destroyed it with megalomanical over-reach into bio-engineered crops; whose influence-peddling rampages constitute some of the slimiest pages in the history of the Clinton administration; whose technological toolkit in the form of Bt corn has threatened to wipe out the Monarch butterfly.

Friedman is so marinated in self-regard that he doesn't even know when he's being stupid. "While the defining measurement of the Cold War was weight — particularly the throw weight of missiles — the defining measurement of the globalization system is speed..." Sounds good in a corporate round-table, means nothing. The man just isn't that smart, beyond the dubious ability to make money out of press releases praising globalism and American power.

With less incoherent choler other reporters and columnists made haste to rustle up uplifting parables about the benefits of "free trade" — standard shorthand for the ability of global capital, led by the US, to roam and pillage at will. Typical was "Carrying the Flag for Free Trade: Brazil Still Embraces Globalization" by Simon Romero, published by the New York Times on December 2, 1999. "Brazil", Romero asserted, "points to itself as an example of the positive economic change that can come from policies advocated by the 135-nation group [the WTO]."

If Romero had bothered to study the chart accompanying his own article, he would have seen that Brazil's per capita GDP growth has averaged approximately 2.5 percent annually over the last decade. But data from the United Nations show that Brazil's per capita GDP growth averaged 4.7 percent annually in the period from 1960 to 1980, when it was following a more inward-looking path to development. At one point the article notes that Brazil is still a relatively closed economy, and points out that other nations, such as Mexico, are much more integrated into the world economy. It comments on this point: "Brazil has a long way to go before thoroughly reaping the rewards of free trade." Data from the IMF, show that over the last 15 years Mexico's per capita GDP growth has averaged approximately 1.0 percent annually.

Time and again the journalistic barkers for the WTO

insisted that increased trade results in better jobs for workers."
As the economist Dean Baker pointed out, this is a serious
misrepresentation of standard economic theory on trade, which
"implies that increased trade can on average raise living
standards, but that there will also be winners and losers from
increased trade. It is entirely possible that much of the
workforce, possibly even a majority, could see their wages
depressed as a result of international competition. It is also
worth noting that according to economic theory, extending
barriers like patents and copyright protection, which has also
been part of the WTO agenda, could lower living standards
worldwide. The vast majority of workers who hold jobs in an
export industry would have also held jobs had those exports not
existed, just as the vast majority of workers who lose jobs due
to imports will find alternative employment. Whether trade has
on net benefited a particular group of workers will depend on
whether it has led to an increase in demand for their specific
skills."

NBC's financial correspondent Mike Jensen extolled the
benefits of free trade and concluded that "most experts say
getting rid of trade barriers on both sides is a good thing for
American workers and consumers. But no matter what comes
out of this four-day meeting — and a lot of analysts don't think
it will be much—world trade has such momentum, almost
nothing can get in its way." Yet, as Dean Baker points out, there
is "near consensus among economists that trade has been one of
the factors that has increased wage inequality in the United

States over the last two decades." But that "consensus" is decidedly harder to find in mainstream press accounts.

An amusing example of the indignation with which much of the corporate press viewed the WTO protests came with the announcement by (Disney-owned) ABC's Seattle affiliate that it would "not devote coverage to irresponsible or illegal activities of disruptive groups", adding that "KOMO 4 News is taking a stand on not giving some protest groups the publicity they want.... So if you see us doing a story on a disruption, but we don't name the group or the cause, you'll know why." In a revealing choice of words, KOMO's news director Joe Barnes described civil disobedience as "illegally disrupting the commerce of the city".

But the press also blacked out less militant opponents of the WTO such as Ralph Nader. His Citizens' Trade Campaign, under the direction of Lori Wallach, put on a week's worth of teach-ins which were ignored by the corporate scriveners as resolutely as though they had been training schools for making Molotov cocktails.

But criticism of the street warriors was not confined to the corporate custodians of "free market" commercial morality. Here was the line-up on this important battleground. On the one side: lib-lab pundits, flacks for John Sweeney and James Hoffa like the Nation's Marc Cooper, Molly Ivins and Jim Hightower, middle-of-the road greens, Michael Moore, a recycle binful of policy wonks from the Economic Policy Institute and kindred DC think-tanks, Doug Tompkins (the former czar of sweatshop-made sports clothing who funds the International Forum on Globalization), Medea Benjamin (empress of Global Exchange). On the other side: the true heroes of the Battle in Seattle — the street warriors, the Ruckus Society, the Anarchists, Earth First!ers, anti biotech activists, French farmers, radical labor militants such as the folks at Jobs With Justice, hundreds of Longshoremen, Steelworkers, Electrical Workers and Teamsters who disgustedly abandoned the respectable, police-sanctioned official AFL-CIO parade and joined the street warriors at the barricades in downtown.

At issue here was the liberals' craving to fortify the quasi-myth of Labor Revived — a "progressive coalition" of John Sweeney's AFL-CIO, Hoffa's Teamsters, mainstream greens — poised and ready to recapture the soul of the Democratic Party. The way they spun it, the collapse of the WTO talks in Seattle was a glorious triumph for respectable demonstrators, achieved despite the pernicious rabble smashing windows, harassing the police and bringing peaceful mainstream protest into disrepute.

Listen to Ivins: "Of those 35,000 people, fewer than 1,000 misbehaved by trashing some local stores. How much more coverage do the 1,000 who misbehaved get than the 34,000 who didn't? A. 35 times as much? B. 34 times as much? C. Virtually all the coverage? You are correct: C is the answer. Do the other 34,000 people get any coverage? Yes — they are referred to as 'some people concerned about the turtles'... Meanwhile the violent protesters are interviewed on national television, identify themselves as anarchists and explain to us all that owning property is wrong and that none of the earth should be in private hands."

Carl Pope, executive director of the Sierra Club, took a similar tack in an internal memo to his board of directors: "The Sierra Club was completely separate from the illegal protest, both violent and non-violent..." Pope went on to quote Kathleen Casey, one of his staffers, to the effect that "The new coalition that worked together to thwart the WTO came out a clear winner. The Sierra Club achieved many of our goals despite the chaos and unfortunate violence that occurred in some of the actions... Some small factions engaged in vandalism and provocation, and the police sometimes over-reacted in kind."

The Nation's Marc Cooper announced tremulously that "the media focus on a few broken store windows should not distract from the profundity of what has happened here..." Cooper evoked "a phantasmagorical mix of tens of thousands of peaceful demonstrators... something not seen since the sixties, but in [its] totality unimaginable even then." And what this "unimaginable" thing? "The rough outlines of the much-sought-after progressive coalition — an American version of a 'red-green' alliance."

In the fervid imagination of Michael Moore the union protests in Seattle had an effect on President Bill Clinton akin to that exercised by Jesus Christ on St Paul on the Damascus road. In a binding curve of liberal hagiography Moore managed to conflate Christ, Clinton, Paul and JFK,: "He [Clinton] completely changed his position [he didn't] and called on all WTO countries to enact laws prohibiting trade with nations that use children in sweatshops and do not honor the rights of all workers to organize a union. Whoa!... So, for Clinton to climb the space needle (or was he chased up it?) and then declare [he didn't] that the human rights of workers were more important than making a buck, well, this was nothing short of Paul being knocked off his horse and seeing Jesus [he didn't]!...You could almost hear the collective seething of the hundreds of CEOs gathered in Seattle. Their boy Bill — the politician they had bought and paid for ... had betrayed them. You could almost see them reaching for their Palm Pilots to look up the phone number of The Jackal."

To concoct the myth of respectable triumph in Seattle, divorced from dreadlocked and locked-down Earth First!-ers, turbulent Ruckusites been and kindred rabble, the respectable liberals tortured the data to produce the following entirely fictitious version of what happened in Seattle. Initial scouting parties of liberal policy wonks arrived in Seattle over the weekend prior to the WTO assembly and embarked on a series of (sleep-inducing) debates and panels, chewing over the minutiae of proposed WTO rules and regulations. As originally envisaged, these moots were scheduled to last all week, until by a process of inexorable erosion, like the Colorado river gradually cleaving its way through the Navajo sandstone to create the Grand Canyon, the WTO would be transmuted into a wholesome compact between First World and Third, between mighty corporations and African peasants, Nike and starving Indonesian workers to the betterment of all.

Then, the liberal fantasy continued, on Monday battalions of clean-limbed environmentalists in their turtle necks and turtle costumes moved in disciplined array to a (police-approved) rallying spot where they were uplifted by the measured words of that Pericles of mainstream greenery, Carl Pope. After the speechifying, the battalions redeployed in the Methodist church on Fifth St which sheltered the command and control center of the progressive Non-Governmental Organizations, aka NGOs. (In foundation-funded political wonkdom the acronym "NGO" is used constantly, often in conjunction with the phrase "civil society", to evoke non-profit organizations that mediate the public interest with governments. Oxfam is an NGO. The Interfaith Council is an NGO. World Wildlife Fund is an NGO.)

Down in the basement of the church and indeed rarely emerging into the light of day was Jim Hightower, the faux-populist icon of Austin, Radio Nation's Marc Cooper and other communicators. Upstairs were the briefing rooms and mock tribunals in more or less permanent session.

In this fantasy version of history the official finale was the great labor march of Tuesday, November 30, when some 25,000 union people rallied under the indulgent eyes of the Seattle constabulary in an old football stadium, to listen to John Sweeney, James P. Hoffa of the Teamsters and such labor chieftains as Gerald McEntee of the AFSCME. The divorce of rhetoric from reality was best represented by McEntee who appropriated Carl Oglesby's famous line from the 1960s, "We have to name the system". Unlike Oglesby, who was a genuinely radical SDS leader, McEntee (annual salary in excess of $300,000) has been among the most fervent of all Big Labor's supporters of Clinton-Gore.

The rally over, Sweeney and Hoffa led their thousands towards downtown where, as was noted in St Clair's battlefront diary, at that precise moment the street warriors were desperately but successfully preventing delegates from entering the Convention Center and Paramount theater where the opening ceremony was scheduled to take place. It was touch and go as cops steadily got rougher and the tear gas got thicker. Certainly the arrival of thousands of labor marchers on the scene would have made it much more difficult for the cops to gas, beat and shoot the activists with wooden plugs and rubber bullets. It would have diminished the hundreds of serious injuries sustained by the street warriors.

The labor marchers approached and then... their own marshals turned them back. A few rebellious steelworkers, longshoremen, electrical workers and teamsters did disobey their leaders, push into downtown and join the battle. The main march withdrew in respectable good order and the demonstrators dispersed peacefully to their hotels, where Molly Ivins and the other scriveners began composing their denunciations of the anarcho-trashers who had marred the great event.

It would no doubt be polite to treat this myth-making as contemptible but harmless. But real social movements for change shouldn't be built on illusions, and the self-aggrandizement was far from harmless. Take Medea Benjamin of Global Exchange, an NGO that has made its name on the sweatshop issue, dickering with Nike over the pay rates and factory conditions of its workers in Vietnam, Indonesia and China. Whatever cachet Benjamin might have won by sneaking into a WTO session and being arrested and briefly addressing the delegates was swiftly squandered by her subsequent deeds, defending Niketown. Benjamin and her Global Exchange cohorts stood on the steps of Niketown and sweatshop outlets in downtown Seattle to defend the premises against demonstrators. The New York Times quoted Benjamin as saying: "Here we are protecting Nike, McDonalds, the GAP and all the while I'm thinking, 'Where are the police? These anarchists should have been arrested."

In an account of her actions addressed to members of Global Exchange, Benjamin refined her position: "Did Global Exchange take the position, as Founding Director Medea Benjamin was in The New York Times, that those engaged in property destruction should be arrested? When asked by a reporter what she thought the police should do with those who were destroying property, Medea responded rather matter-of-factly, 'arrest them'". Then Benjamin added testily in her account, "Many of the key organizers of the protest had interviews set up with national media that were cancelled at the last minute because the media preferred to cover 'the anarchists'". Note the tone of injured self-importance, as though the inconvenience of her missing an appointment with a television producer or some hack like Friedman was more important than the attack on Niketown.

The larger political agenda of the liberals with their myth-making was far from benign. By falsely proclaiming a victory for peaceful pro-cop protesters marshalled under the banners of the AFL-CIO, they were preparing, under a largely factitious banner of "unity", to hunker down with the government policy makers to rewrite the WTO treaty to their satisfaction. This is the core meaning of co-option, and certainly the London Economist understood it well enough. In the wake of Seattle the Economist ran a long article discussing the rising power of NGOs, which successfully challenged the World Bank, sank the Multilateral Agreement on Investment and engineered the anti-landmine campaign. But, the Economist continued, there's hope. "Take the case of the World Bank. The 'Fifty Years is Enough' campaign of 1994 was a prototype of Seattle (complete with activists invading the meeting halls). Now the NGOs are surprisingly quiet about the World Bank. The reason is that the Bank has made a huge effort to coopt them." The Economist went on to describe how World Bank president James Wolfensohn had given the NGOs a seat at the table, and now more than 70 NGO policy wonks work in the Bank's offices world-wide, and half of the bank's projects have some NGO involvement.

No one should look at the NGOs without first reading Michel Foucault on co-option and internalisation of the disciplinary function. NGOs are often invoked by their admirers as sterling exemplars of the vitality of civil society. But as Tessa

Morris-Suzuki pointed out in New Left Review (March/April 2000), the rise of NGOs mime the spread of neo-liberal policies as "states shift responsibility for some of their social and welfare functions to private or volunteer groups." So one can readily appreciate why institutions like the World Bank can easily appropriate the argot of emancipation and the cachet of NGOs as the cutting edge of "new social movements". NGOs can be instruments of "good governance". As Morris-Suzuki aptly remarks, "The fact that social movements are 'non-governmental' or that they operate multiversally does not guarantee that they will work in favor of the marginalized and disadvantaged. Their motive can be equally well to guard established preserves of power and privilege from those who demand to share them; their energies may be mobilized by governments or state agencies — like the US military — to prop up existing structures of power." Many NGO functionaries, for example, supported the US-dominated intervention in Somalia and Yugoslavia.

In 1998 the Rand Arroyo Center, a research group affiliated to the US Army, published a report entitled "The Zapatista 'Social Netwar in Mexico'. The document (cited by Morris-Suzuki) was sponsored by the US Army's Deputy Chief of Staff for Intelligence. It discussed how to counter the Zapatistas' success in evolving "network forms of organization, doctrine, strategy, and technology attuned to the information age" that represent an "epistemological" challenge to imperial counter-insurgency. As part of this challenge the Army Intelligence report cited the internet, obviously enough, but it is also focussed on NGOs and recommended that "where feasible, it may be increasingly advisable to improve US and allied skills for communication and even coordination with NGOs that can affect the course and conduct of a netwar". Anyone wanting an illustration of how that recommendation has been taken seriously need only study the role "human rights" NGOs like Amnesty International and Human Rights Watch have on occasion helped justify US imperial policies in venues as various as Iraq and Colombia.

Finally, the myth-making about Seattle actively demobilizes radical struggles against the two party status quo, since it pretends that one of the two parties — the Democrats, naturally — can actually be redeemed.

But it's all a myth, which can be easily popped with a simple question: if labor's legions had not shown up in Seattle the direct action protesters would have at least succeeded in shutting down the opening session on Tuesday, November 30, and they conceivably could have dominated the agenda of the entire week, as in fact they did. If the direct action protesters had not put their bodies on the line throughout that entire week, if the only protest had been that under official AFL-CIO banners, then there would have been a 15-second image of a parade on the national news headlines that Tuesday evening and that would have been it. The WTO would have gone forward with barely a ripple of discord except for what the African and Caribbean nations had managed to foment from the inside.

Remember, after Tuesday most of the labor people had gone back to work, and the street warriors were on their own, prompting the Seattle police finally to overreach and go berserk to such a degree that the people of Seattle and the press turned against them. People like Moore and Ivins should have been taking up the cause of those protesters still facing charges. They should also have been pinning the blame on those who told the cops to take the gloves off. By Tuesday night both the White House and the US Justice Department were telling the mayor of Seattle that Clinton would not come if the streets weren't cleared. Attorney General Janet Reno wanted the feds to take over the policing actions, which almost certainly would have led to a massacre.

Contrast the outlook of Benjamin and the other protectors of corporate property with the attitude of a 34-year old Oregon farmer who found himself in the midst of the downtown protest, was arrested and harshly treated in jail: "To break a window in a retail facility in downtown Seattle is nothing compared to what some of these CEOs are doing daily."

Or listen to Jeff Crosby, the president of a union local of International Union of Electrical Workers who flew to Seattle with 15 of his fellow union members from New England. Crosby works at a GE plant, which is about to relocate in Mexico. After he went home, Crosby put up on the web this open letter: "The decision by the AFL-CIO not to plan direct action was a mistake. The literature and petition the AFL-CIO used for Seattle was mostly unreadable and unusable, with no edge. Despite some heroic efforts by union folks in Seattle and other places, the AFL-CIO campaign was reminiscent of the 'old' AFL-CIO's campaign against NAFTA — remember 'Not This NAFTA'? If we had run a campaign against the congressional 'Fast Track' vote with 'Not this fast-track', we would have lost that one too. Did anyone really try to bring people to Seattle under the slogan, 'We demand a working group'?

"This is a period when on certain issues, massive, non-violent direct action is in order, as the demonstration in Seattle shows. Every member who went on our trip reports that support for the demonstrations, even with the disruptions, is overwhelming. And not just from other workers in the shop, but family and other friends, regardless of what they do for a living. 'Since we came home, we're being treated like conquering heroes,' marveled one of our group.

"Perhaps the AFL-CIO was driven by policy advisers in Washington who didn't understand how angry people are about this issue... Perhaps they did not want to embarrass Gore. Perhaps Sweeney had an agreement with Clinton to ask for enforcible labor standards. Perhaps they thought that most people would be turned off by civil disobedience, or something else, I don't know. There were plenty of people in the labor movement pushing for the labor movement to join in the Direct Action — we lost."

Fortunately the street people won.

Chapter 4

JoAnn Wypijewski's DC Diary: April Was a Jolly Month

Sometime around 8 am on Monday, April 17, about twenty Metro DC police in modified riot gear posed in front of the White House while two of their fellow officers snapped their pictures. This was Day 2 of mass protests against the IMF and the World Bank, and the closest anyone would come that day to a tourist moment in a city usually crawling with tourists. Across the faces in blue were the dubious smiles of an even more dubious victory. Here was the power core of downtown Washington vacant and militarized; the Treasury and Commerce departments locked tight, along with State, Interior, the General Services Administration, the federal Office of Personnel Management and almost every other office and store in a thirteen-by-eight-block area. Here was the lobbyist corridor of K Street desolate, no phones ringing, or palms greased, or promises greedily made. "We didn't lose the city", Police Chief Charles Ramsey would say later, and, taking note, the next day's morning papers would say the demonstrators had "failed".

Unlike the WTO conclave in Seattle, the spring meetings of the IMF and World Bank proceeded more or less on schedule (even if other business at those institutions was thwarted, all but employees essential to the meetings having been told to stay home). And Washington never became an all-out war zone. The police ($5 million in overtime, $1 million in new riot equipment), the National Guard, US Marshals and about twenty other security forces at varying stages of readiness — together, they had shut down the city in order to save it.

Uniformly, the big media led their reports of A16 (tag for the two-day protest beginning April 16) with images of policemen beating, gassing and otherwise manhandling young counter-culture demonstrators. Liberals love this sort of thing; it allows them, simultaneously, to write off the radicals as near-hoodlums acting out individual, as opposed to collective, passions and to disdain some cops as thugs. (It's the old "extremes of both sides" formula, expressed in all its unselfconscious nuttiness by the Washington Times, to wit, "The protesters were concerned about police batons, gas masks and pepper-spray guns, and the officers became concerned when they saw protesters donning goggles and bandannas for protection.") Where the demonstrators weren't drawn as mindless children bored with privilege, they were victims. Either way, they were powerless.

But if victory is measured in offensive power at the scene of protest, then the Radical Cheerleaders from American University ("J-U-S-T-I-C-E, Justice, Justice will set us free!"), the magical puppets from Vermont, the spooky black bloc of anarchists and the hundreds of other affinity groups from all over the country that made up the direct-action faction of the

Mobilization for Global Justice had it all over the police. The latter managed to defend their positions only by the threat, and occasional use, of heavy arms and chemical agents. By their own admission, they never knew where the demonstrators would be coming from next. Like a disciplined many-headed guerrilla squad — it's too early to speak of armies — different groups took one intersection, marched to another, rounded the corner of a third. They had determined their positions days before, had modified those as they got new intelligence, had defined the roles of "arrestables" and "nonarrestables", had delegated their own medical and legal attendants, had formed rapid-response teams and tactical alliances linking affinity groups to clusters, to super-clusters, and on to groups in the permitted march and rally on Sunday. Shank the Bank, the affinity group out of Seattle that adopted me, agreed to back up the position of the Friends of Fucking Florida and a Missouri group at 5 AM on Sunday, before making the procession to the area anchored by its super-cluster, Radical Alliance, a little while later.

Beginning at about 11 or so, a group of us would move back and forth between the direct action near the IMF and World Bank buildings and the rally nearby at the Ellipse.) The black bloc, moving purposefully under its black and red flags, often in near silence ("Where do you come from?" "From out of hiding"), scuffled with police from time to time but it defined its chief mission as the protection and defense of the main body of protesters. Many times during the day police donned their gas masks and advanced; many times our lines grew more defiant, more jubilant. People appeared out of nowhere passing around baggies of vinegar for soaking bandannas against the possible gas attack. The chants grew more exuberant; the cops backed down. The cry went up: "Ain't no power like the power of the people, 'cause the power of the people don't stop." This happened easily as many times as, and possibly more often than, the violent assaults by police. One tense face-off on Monday between police and a small group from the black bloc dissolved when the protesters tossed marshmallow Peeps, perennial Easter-basket favorite, in the cops' direction, calling out "Power to the Peeps!" The police retreated in laughter. "Let's never lose our sense of the ridiculous", said one of the participants.

Those April days in Washington brought together many skeins of organization: the Fifty Years Is Enough campaign against the World Bank (originally a project of the International Rivers Network); Jubilee 2000, the international campaign to cancel Third World debt; Ralph Nader's various anti-trade coalitions and his followers in the Green Party; the blocs of black-clad anarchist still fervid from Seattle; the Direct Action Network; various grads of Ruckus Society training camps; the Zap the Gap group from Northern California which brought back streaking to the nation's capital; student organizers of the anti-sweat shop movement; labor militants.

No one, least of all the demonstrators, should have really expected that we could have prevented the IMF/WB meeting from happening. The coordinators of the direct-action faction had essentially taken the plan from Seattle as a template for

Washington. It was a strategic error. Police habituated to protecting presidents are far more controlling, and controlled, than those accustomed to protecting Starbucks — neither side even bothered with Starbucks in DC — and the cops too had studied the tapes from Seattle. The father of a Maryland State Trooper, one of the units mobilized for A16, told me his son was part of a team that had been taken to Atlanta for such video review and riot training and while there was given the instruction that should things get dangerously out of hand, "don't worry about anything; shoot to kill". The father was a union man who supported the broad aims of the protest.

In DC the police would strike first. Early in the morning on the day before the protest, they raided the Convergence Center, locus for the Direct Action Network and strategic hub/support link for everyone mustered to block the meetings. In front of the police barrier, a kid held a sign saying "Excuse the delay. State repression underway". The center never reopened. Late that afternoon police conducted what might be called an exemplary arrest, encircling about 600 people—most of them protesters marching from a mini-rally for Mumia and against police violence, but also tourists, journalists and passers-by who hadn't quite passed by — then hauling them off to jail.

To anyone arriving in Washington days before the protest, observing police fortifications and aware that there weren't the numbers to block delegates at the point of departure (their hotels) as well as arrival (IMF/WB headquarters), it was clear that "Shut them down!" would be less a practical exhortation than an expression of political will. Afterward there would be complaints among some of the protesters that it was a tactical error to maintain the cry if the objective was impossible; that there had been no flexibility to consider other ways a shut-down might have been possible; that something was amiss organizationally when there were no back-up plans, "and back-up plans to the back-up plans". But simply on the basis of things as they were, if victory is to be measured in moral power, then the defensive bleats of the IMF/WB delegates about defeating poverty and pulling up those countries that have been "left behind" by the worldwide capitalist bonanza marked another success for the protesters.

It's all a liberal feint, of course. No one came out to announce that the debt was canceled in, say, Brazil, which the World Bank applauds for identifying "'social justice' as a priority" but which had to spend $216 billion servicing the external debt between 1989 and 1997, and even then still owed $212 billion. (On the same day it was reporting on the protests, the Washington Post ran a moist story about staggering rates of alcoholism among Brazil's Maxakali Indians. Though they are "economically paralyzed, socially isolated and politically invisible", the writer concluded comfortably that "denial may actually be their biggest problem".)

But the moral argument never was intended for the delegates. As in Seattle with the WTO, A16 put the issues of debt, "structural adjustment" and the worldwide transfer of wealth from the poor to the rich on the public radar screen.

Hostile commentators have got a lot of mileage out of the idea that this was a protest without a cause, or with too many causes to make sense of; that we're all "global village idiots", as the Wall Street Journal noted, without the clarity of the now-sentimentalized sixties antiwar protesters. But debt slavery is not a hard thing to grasp for most people with too many credit cards and too many loans. And "Cancel the debt" is no less pithy than "Stop the war".

It's a journalistic cliche to take the temperature of a town by its taxi drivers, but again and again immigrant drivers hailed the protesters for bringing their countries' woes to light. "What is going on is simply the recolonization of the so-called developing world, and until now how many Americans even heard of the IMF?" said a driver from Ethiopia (total debt 1996, $10 billion; debt per person, $173; GNP per person, $102). "This is why we are taxi drivers", said a former car dealer from Nigeria (total debt 1996, $31.4 billion; debt per person, $275; GNP per person, $272). The best measure of victory, though, would totally elude the big (and even small "progressive") media. That's the degree to which a particular action moves opposition closer to movement — not notionally but tactically. Coming out of Seattle there was an irritating game being played among defiants, a kind of one-upmanship of suffering, or perhaps machismo? Outside a planning meeting of the direct-action faction at the Calvary Baptist Church the Friday before A16, one guy who'd been in Seattle asked another if he'd been gassed there. "Hell, yes, three times." To which the first guy replied, "I got hit, like, five times." For others it was seven, or nine or — God help you — not at all.

After Seattle there was also a lot of inflated talk about the Red-Green alliance (now modified to Blue-Green; someone noticed that organized labor is not exactly the IWW), but the crucial division was always between the kids et al. seizing the streets and the big institutions (notably labor) marching safely: illegal and legal, mutually sympathetic (broadly speaking) but mostly separate and certainly unequal, certainly suspicious of each other. Washington was different. Contrary to some grumblers, it was a very good thing that the AFL-CIO didn't come into the coalition sponsoring the permitted march and rally until very late. It couldn't claim turf privilege. There wouldn't be an advance guard of burly Machinists marking the march route, as there had been in Seattle, and there wouldn't be endless talk of "working groups", of responsible and irresponsible protesters, of "Teamsters and Turtles, Together at Last", the wistful mantra from Seattle that obscured as much, if not more than it revealed. But it was a good thing that at least a fragment of labor did come into the coalition.

There had been talk of "tens of thousands" of expected participants in the permitted events with almost nothing to back up the prediction. (In the end, the total number of protesters for the weekend was somewhere between 15,000 and 20,000. The DC police don't do protest counts anymore.) They had five walkie-talkies instead of thirty-five, a dozen "peacekeepers" for the march instead of about 250 (most of them tenacious young women who maintained the line of march without being bullies), no working alliance with the direct-action faction, no clear plan even for building the stage. It wasn't until April 12 that an Ironworkers local committed about ten volunteers for the task and arranged for the heavy equipment. Stage-building night, which commenced about twelve hours before the rally was set to begin, said it all, as AFL people were laying planks for the forklift and hauling scaffolding while the putative organizer of the stage crew was driving around to Home Depot.

What labor participation there was for A/16 came through the agency of Jobs With Justice, the nationwide labor-community coalition with its own tradition of direct action. As Simon Greer, JWJ's chief tactician for A16 and liaison to the direct-action faction, put it, "The breakthrough idea from Seattle was 'We're not all special interests; we're in this together.' But quickly that rhetorical enthusiasm dissipated." By March it looked as though almost no one would be together for the April events. The advocates of debt forgiveness for the Third World (Jubilee 2000) had their day on April 9. The AFL would thunder away at China on April 12, bringing some 10,000 unionists to town to lobby against permanent normal trade relations and offering up a stew of human rights and, especially from the Steelworkers' George Becker, foam-flecked anticommunism. Everyone else was coming to town for the 16th, and even before they converged no one would remember the rest. The AFL wasn't interested in A16 — too symbolic, too exhausting on the members, too potentially out of control. But random activists, trade unionists, union staff began pressing Jobs With Justice. The "movement", such as it is, was coming to town, and where was labor? The Naderites and their allies had been calling unions cold to try to get them on board for the rally, but without relationships to those unions they got nowhere.

Three weeks before A16, two staff members of the AFL's department of field mobilization, one of them with a long JWJ history, put the case to the federation: ignoring the protest would be suicidal for future alliances, and in any case would be politically derelict. Jobs With Justice would be the pivot. It got the Steelworkers and six other unions to sign on. In the end, the federation moved, nervously. Could JWJ get the numbers? Could it guarantee safety for thousands of people who wouldn't be coming to break the law? This was a new thing for the AFL to be in a supporting role. Earlier I'd asked an AFL official what would count as a disaster for the AFL on A16. "Oh, if Gerry McEntee [AFSCME's president] gets arrested, I think that would pretty much be it." However much top union leaders may speechify against capitalism, they have a stake in playing by the rules.

Partly because it was late but also because the people at Jobs With Justice have a far different orientation from the bureaucrats, the tactics of labor had to be totally different from those of Seattle. Coordination with the direct action people was essential. The question, Greer says, was how would the march relate to the direct action not how separate can they keep things "Our main issues, which we told the DAN folks, were, first, that we had no moral imperative to take any particular street. If you block F, we'll take E. We ended up marching on none of the streets permitted. And, second, that we had a moral obligation to the marchers' safety."

The view of many after Seattle was that labor had betrayed our side when John Sweeney failed to lead 25,000 marchers into gas-laden streets. It's nice to imagine that the AFL might ever be such a militant institution, but quite apart from Sweeney's priorities, the fact is that most of those 25,000 people didn't come to Seattle to be gassed; and in most protest situations there will be masses of people who are passionate to participate but aren't ready to flout the law and aren't willing to risk their safety.

For A16, Greer and the others decided that solidarity was crucial but that if there was any hope of drawing unions into closer relationship with direct-action forces in the future, peacekeeping here would be the key. And not just for those anxiously sitting at AFL HQ. "Philadelphia ACT-UP brought 800 people with HIV or AIDS", Greer noted by way of example, "and we made a promise to them that so far as we could help it, they wouldn't wind up in jail or be hurt." So the peacekeepers were trained and given their orders, but Greer was also on the direct-action faction's communication system.

On Sunday, people flowed in and out of the rally and back to the streets. The Ellipse had the feel of a love-in for the presence of the kids, and when things were getting hot on the periphery, people could hear it and they could move. (They were not, needless to say, directed to do so from the stage.) The main medical team for the protesters was situated at the home of SEIU Local 82, which was also the place where the puppet-making moved after police had shut down the Convergence Center. When it came time for the march to begin, the peacekeepers held back the designated front line of the march to let the puppets lead the way. It was called "the labor march", but it didn't look it, and when people peeled away to move toward streets being held by affinity groups, by and large the peacekeepers weren't obstructive.

Partway through the march the direct-action faction's coordinators decided that it would be tactically smart for everyone to merge into the march anyway: victory could be declared, the street action wouldn't be left to fizzle out. The police never quite knew where the march would turn, but except in a couple of instances, they didn't threaten it. Ultimately, even the black bloc entered the Ellipse. None of this means there was no tension between the various factions (even within factions), or that we've arrived at some movement launchpad. This was one action, and while tactics can foster trust and unity of purpose, eventually politics will intrude (though it may take some time for those to be defined).

Right now, there are contradictions galore. THE AFL took its lead from Jobs With Justice this time around, but it's still an establishment institution , not structured for risk or radicalism. George Becker's enthusiasm for A16 turned out to be as fiery as his anticommunism, and for the same reason. Like a lot of unionists, he wants to protect jobs and he is moved by stories of exploitation and injustice. But he views the world the way labor has for decades, and it's a perspective that not only continues to dog US labor's relationships with unions internationally but also places labor in a different universe from its young A16 allies. It's far from clear whether such alliances will ever extend beyond a particular agreed-upon action.

Labor made a certain commitment to A16.. On the 17th, when a few thousand protesters braved a numbing rain ("We're here, we're wet; cancel the debt") and many more police, they were once again alone. And the day after that, when 600 to 700 people were in jail and reports from inside were hair-raising, the Metro labor council called the city council to complain but didn't bring any more power to bear, nor was it asked to.

The biggest arrest of the weekend was a brokered one: in return for a police stand-down from their posture of imminent violent assault on April 17, about 500 protesters would let the police deny them their freedom. I've never thought much of choreographed arrests, but the image of waves of people, many soaked to the skin, putting it all on the line was very powerful. To the labor crowd, civil disobedience is understandable, but the protesters' ethic of "jail solidarity", by which arrestees refuse to cooperate with authorities and hold to their cells until everyone is released, is beyond them. There may be arguments about the efficacy of such a jail strategy, but it's the hard stuff that is the test of an alliance, and labor might note that there's not much of a step from jail solidarity to "An injury to one is an injury to all".

Jeff Engels, of the Inland Boatman's Union/ILWU and the

Seattle affinity group, has been telling his comrades that if they want a real movement they've got to make room for people who aren't like them. Organizationally, they'll have to figure out how to have consensus (a group ethic even more powerful than jail solidarity) and accountable leadership, how to have a structure that is decentralized but still lets people find out what's going on, and how to engage people who might not have a computer or might not be able to spend four hours at a meeting.

These are, needless to say, old questions in a new frame. But it's exciting to be asking them again, and not only as a theoretical exercise.

Part 2

Laura Flanders' DC Diary: How IndyMedia Was Born

If my cellphone had a hook, it would have been ringing off it: "There's tear gas outside the Treasury...the press conference is at 4.00...the FCC are right outside..." Throughout the days of protest in Washington DC, the phonecalls from the Independent Media Center (IMC) came in breathless, by the hour. Photographs and eyewitness bulletins were there for the taking on the internet, and in parts of DC you could tune into Mobilization Radio, an unlicensed micro-station, which emitted stream-of-consciousness broadcasts from various undisclosed locations until the FCC shut it down.

Unlike many a DC rally, the anti-capitalist action in the capitol was not laid on primarily to play to CNN's anchors: there were no sound-bite-ready official spokespeople, few celebrities, no press kits, not even a predictable march route. But that doesn't mean that A16 was media-unfriendly: far from it. Communications-savvy activists worked every technology at their disposal and those who were in the loop got all the news, up to the latest burst of pepper-spray. On the web, the IMC is at www.indymedia.org. Its non-virtual home in DC was a whitewashed art gallery on 9th and N (a friendly, disheveled part of town.)

By April 15, some 1000 volunteer media-makers had registered to play their part. Up a ladder, on a storage shelf-turned studio, camera-people shot interviews. Barely a week later, a video documentary was available via satellite for public access cable stations (and others) to broadcast. (See www.papertiger.org.) In a sound-proof walk-in closet, audio techies bounced the sound from the streets, via palm-size recorders, onto laptop computers, to the web, for far-off community radio stations to downloaded and play on-air. The old-media folks faced a temporary crisis. Smack in the middle of going to press with the "Blind Spot" (the IMC's four-page broadsheet) the in-house copier crashed, and three nearby Kinko shops — the 24-hour standby of pamphlet-printers everywhere — shut down, citing "riot activity." "The employee was polite as he asked us to leave," reported Troy Skeels for the IMC, "but explained that our presence was putting his shop in danger of being closed due to police pressure."

With no riot in sight, Skeels and friends hiked to Georgetown, and produced several thousand copies of BLIND SPOT there instead. There was a reunion of sorts on the streets of the city. In Chicago, at the 1996 Democratic Convention, DC's chief of police Charles Ramsey, was deputy commander of the Chicago police department. The "protest pit" strategy his forces used there greeted activists again in Washington. Relying on heavy cop presence and barricades to block all access to the DNC in Chicago, Ramsey's forces fenced critics into "free speech" zones — parking lots miles from the site. He was trying, no doubt, to prevent another '68 debacle (when police riots made it onto network television).

What happened (among other things) was that media activists were inspired to collaborate and what was to become the IMC was born. To get as much information out as widely as they could, given minimal access and maximum constraint, reporters from different media shared resources, ability and energy, to cover what was not in the mainstream and put the info out into the world wide web. "Not as many people looked, four years ago," said Jay Sands, one of the group's many coordinators. But Indymedia took off in Seattle and the habit is catching on: in Philadelphia and Los Angeles for the major party conventions and in Melbourne for the world economic conference. For many the world wide web was the only to see what happened when thousands confronted the IMF at its annual meeting in Prague in September, 2000.

Initiatives like the under-funded, overstretched, IMC collective may not solve the media-access problem, but they sure can help. When Mobilization Radio, the low-watt station that covered the protest, announced that the FCC were at the door to shut them down, three hundred demonstrators arrived on the scene in minutes. "What happened next was probably unprecedented in the history of microradio", wrote Joe Tuba, for the IMC. Apparently taken aback by the crowd, the police, FBI, FCC and assorted other intelligence left the scene without making arrests or grabbing equipment. "The crowd immediately took the street in celebration..." Tuba went on, "and the station was disassembled and carried out as the participants left the building and regained anonymity as members of the crowd."

The fun and excitement at the IMC sure beats the dismal drone of the Pacifica wars. One thing is clear: while Pacifica's management and their friends are fiddling, the world of public media burns, which is to say, burns up. Independent media activism is HOT. This month's anti-World Bank and IMF protests showed that.

Chapter 5

LA Diary:
A Field Day for the Heat

The heat in LA was oppressive: both the broiling sun and the omnipresent cops. The combined effect saturated the streets, but didn't quell the protests mounted over four days and nights at the Democratic National Convention. If the tenor of the demonstrations in LA didn't match the fury of Seattle, that was almost certainly part of the plan.

"This week was about issues", said John Sellers, the head of the Ruckus Society, who had only days earlier been released from jail following his bizarre arrest and confinement in Philadelphia. Sellers, an exuberant organizer, had been nabbed off a street corner by Philly cops, stuck in jail on a slate of novel charges, and hit with a $1 million bail. The transparent intent was to keep the maestro of Seattle from heading West and orchestrating havoc in LA. Sellers' attorneys got the bail reduced and their client freed. "It's not about broken shop windows", says Sellers. "What we've seen over the past 8 months is thousands of people jailed for bearing witness to the takeover of our democracy." The Ruckus Society has trained more than 2,000 activists in the rudiments of direct action protest: how to climb trees, block roads, lockdown on doors, eat and shit in extreme situations, scale buildings, deal with cops, minister to the injured, show solidarity in custody and survive in jail. Their intense training sessions are boot camps for hard-core activists. This kind of training and discipline under pressure paid off in Seattle.

Ruckus' Han Shan described the theory behind one of the techniques that most befuddled cops in Seattle and Washington, the Sleeping Dragon or group lockbox. "It's a fortification. It's a way of saying, you won't allow me to be here and you'll beat the crap out of me for being here, but I'm going to become an atom in this human molecule, and so you have to deal with this. On the morning of N30 in Seattle, there were hundreds of people running around with lock boxes on their right arm looking for someone to join up with. It was very, very powerful — these individuals, these 'free radicals' running around in the streets looking to become a molecule. There's real metaphorical power in that. But it's also about strengthening our position when our bodies and our voices aren't given the credence that they should be."

But LA was going to be different than Seattle or Washington. No attempt would be made to shut down the city, block delegates from the convention hall, disrupt the official proceedings. There were logistical reasons for this. The great Seattle coalition had fragmented. Big labor had endorsed Gore. So had the big environmental groups, even Friends of the Earth, the one potential hold out. Many of those on the streets of Seattle and Washington were registered Democrats, blindly hopeful that their party could be redeemed. Some were even ensconced inside the Staples center as delegates. Add to this the sweeping arrests and illegal detentions in Philadelphia during the Republican National Convention had depleted the direct action ranks of some of the movement's most adept organizers.

What was left in LA was the distilled militant core of the new movement: death penalty opponents, radical greens, Naderites, a few dozen Steelworkers and Longshoremen, homeless advocates, agitators for human rights. There was a crazy coherence and palpable message to most of the two dozen rallies and marches that streamed through downtown LA over the course of the week. There were almost too many to keep track of, the themes coming in waves. On Saturday evening People for the Ethical Treatment of Animals dumped a load of hog manure in front of a hotel to protest factory farming. Sunday afternoon saw a rowdy march against the death penalty. Tuesday saw the largest mass arrest, when the police cracked down on a Critical Mass bicycle rally. Later that evening hundreds gathered to protest sanctions against Iraq. Wednesday's focus was on the police, with a rally and civil disobedience action at the notorious Ramparts division of the LAPD. Gay and lesbian protesters staged one of the most creative acts, a mass "kiss in".

So LA was about marches, more than direct action. The marchers were rambunctious, but never threatening. It was almost as if the ad hoc game plan was to entice the LAPD to come unhinged without the least provocation.

Political conventions these days are mainly about image making and fundraising, not the rough-and-tumble politics and platform spats that used to be the marrow of these gatherings. So it was fitting that the first big protest of the week came together on the beach at Santa Monica, beneath the pier, which the DNC had rented for a fundraiser on the eve of the convention honoring Democratic fatcats and corporate honchos, including executives from Raytheon, Arco, Disney and Chevron. The pier was protected by a legion of cops, many of them on horseback, which led to the piquant sight of women in formal gowns tiptoeing around horse dung. More than a thousand protesters showed up, including Doris "Granny D" Haddock, the 90-year-old political activist, who had walked across the nation last year promoting the cause of campaign finance reform.

Early Monday morning about two thousand environ-mentalists and human rights activists mustered in Pershing Square in downtown LA to support the cause of the U'wa Indians of the Colombian rainforests, whose land is being overrun by Occidental Petroleum, a company with deep historical ties to the Gore family. One of the few union leaders to speak at the protest was Dave Campbell of the Oil and Chemical Workers, who lambasted Oxy's anti-labor record at its Long Beach refinery. Campbell also pointed out that from 1981 through 1991 Oxy owned IBP, the huge meatpacking plant notorious for its monopolistic practices, anti-labor stances, abuse of animals and dangerous working conditions.

That first march through the cavernous streets of LA came

to typify much of the street action for much of the week. The protesters carried large puppets and signs, crafted at the Convergence Center, a makeshift protest factory and flophouse, near MacArthur Park. A carnival atmosphere pervaded the crowd as they sang and chanted taunts at Gore. Even the anarchists were on their best behavior. The dreaded Black Bloc marched arm-in-arm down the street, some of them actually singing songs. Of course, the attire of the street warriors made them easy targets for the LAPD riot squads, who shadowed their every step, often outnumbering them by 5 to 1.

Overhead, eight helicopters darted around LA's glossy skyscrapers, battling for the best view of the scene unfolding below.

The Democrats were so desperate to drum up the Hispanic vote that some party planner invited Rudy Gandara and his militant Chicano band, the Chizmosos, to play a set for the delegates as they entered the Staples Center. "The delegates never knew what hit 'em," said Rudy. "First, we were searched and 'sniffed' by the Secret Service and those wacky dogs of theirs. They actually gave a bit of respect, to my boys' amazement. But hey, after they ripped up the van, that's the least they could do. "Anyway, there we go, off into the belly of the beast. It was surreal. We performed on a large stage with a cool PA where all the delegates enter the Staples Center and grab a drink or taco or something before they enter, while being entertained by a gospel choir or Korean ballet dancer or some sort of 'non-threatening entertainment'. Even the Home

Shopping Network was broadcasting, which we interrupted. So I opened with Pachucos Mambo, which they asked me not to play, cut to Pelon, cuca rachas…Gloria…Cannibal and then 'Thank You', the piece I did for the Zapatistas benefit CD with Noam Chomsky. The lyrics are based on William Burroughs' nasty Thanksgiving anti-homily of the same name.

Rudy's "Thank You" is performed to a backing track that's basically the Hendrix version of the "Star Spangled Banner." "Thank you for a continent to be infected with brutal power and corruption / thank you for the work in your kitchens and factories, picking your crops and the courteous cops", Rudy chants. "For cutting your grass, polishing window glass and kissing your asses." But not for long, not that night. "The producer was waving her hands, screaming for me to cut it. So I just turned my back to her while wearing my Virgin de Guadeloupe gold and green lame banda dress shirt and United Farmworkers headband. She finally had the sound and my mike turned off. "The strange thing was after all that, photographers and journalist run up to the stage and ask 'Who are you guys?' We took shots with me wearing my American flag bandanna over my face. It was insane. The delegates were standing with their mouths open. The Chicano and black area workers and bus drivers were groovin' to the whole thing. It was a blast. They got what they deserved."

Monday evening, while Clinton delivered his own political eulogy, Rage Against the Machine played a raucous set for about 15,000 demonstrators outside the Staples center in the "legal protest zone", a parking lot cordoned off by an eight foot tall fence tipped with concertina wire. As part of the preparation for the convention, the LA Department of Public Works had deforested much of the Staples Center grounds, uprooting about 100 trees and shrubs (assuredly the most aesthetic feature of the gaudy convention center). The convention planners argued that the trees might be used as weapons against the police or demonstrators.

Soon after Rage finished a couple of protesters climbed the fence near the Staples center, waving an anarchist flag and taunting the police. The LAPD thereupon gave an order for the crowd to disperse and cut the power to the stage. The crowd booed but began to amble out of the fenced-in lot. Then the cops began showering the fence line with pepper spray, trying, so they claimed, to get the anarchists off the fence. A few bottles and chunks of concrete were tossed back, falling short of the cops and then all hell broke loose.

About a hundred cops on horseback drove into the crowd trampling more than a dozen people. Behind them about 500 cops carrying guns began to strafe the crowd, firing for more than 45 minutes. "We were moving out, doing exactly what they said and they still shot us", Ramon Martinez told us. Ruben, a farmworker organizer from Stockton, was hit four times in the neck and shoulders with rubber bullets. He said that the exit route out of the protest area was blocked by a line of police firing guns, thus the crowd was forced to huddle in the intersection of Figueroa and 11th street as the bullets flew. The demonstrators weren't the only ones shot. More than a dozen journalists were also hit by the LAPD, including TV crews stationed on top of a nearby building.

To prepare ourselves spiritually for the New Prudery, in the form of Gore and Lieberman's attack on Hollywood's debasement of the higher values, we drove to the Getty Center, perched above Interstate 405, in search of cultural filth from earlier epochs. After all, if Gore and Lieberman are going to get serious about moral cleansing, why stop with South Park when the museums are filled with porn and violence? Sure enough, we were hardly inside the Getty Center's gallery of classical antiquities before we were confronted by an amphora depicting satyrs all set to rape a passel of wood nymphs. We can't imagine Senator Lieberman approving that kind of thing, any more than a pretty explicit rendition of bestiality on an adjacent vase, with Leda making half-hearted efforts to repel the swan. Aside from doing a pre-board for Liebermanism, we were excited to get to the new Getty Center designed by Richard Meier and now advertised as one of the glories of American architecture. One certainly couldn't hope for a more sensational site, perched up above the 405 interstate, with the San Gabriels to the north, Babylon/Hollwood away to the east and the Pacific the other way. Meier set off in the right direction, with some buildings faced with blocks of rough surfaced travertine limestone, designed to look like hill fortresses in Italy or North Africa. But this medieval look is shackled to banal modern surface textures, so the end product is an uninspiring blend of airport/

Hyatt/carceral modernism, with the travertine blocks looking like a set left behind by Cecil B. DeMille. The galleries are rather dingily lit in the modern manner. Lieberman would have felt uncomfortable. Here was Jan Steen's "Bathsheeba After the Bath", featuring a slutty girl eagerly preparing for her first interview with King David. Here too Theodore Gericault's Three Lovers, an unabashed and altogether approving portrayal of two girls and a fellow in bed, blissfully ignorant of the Gore-Lieberman menace to their enjoyment only 180 years over the horizon.

The impresarios of both the Democratic and Republican National Committees would do well to visit the Getty Center and study how they stage-managed big events in the old days. Luca Carlevarijs did a couple of paintings of Venetian regattas, one of them with the doge marrying the city to the Adriatic. How nice it would have been to have had Bill landing in a Venetian barge at Santa Monica pier, marrying his party to Hollywood with by symbolically tossing into the polluted waters a copy of the Telecommunications Reform Act of 1996, etched in gold, before repairing to the lovely home of Barbra Streisand, he dressed as Belshazzar and she as Vashti who, you will recall, declined to attend Ahasuerus's revels, thus paving the way for Esther and, ultimately for Joe Lieberman.

On Wednesday, the protests turned on the police, highlighting the LAPD's reign of terror. Several thousand marchers gathered at MacArthur Park early in the morning and walked through the 95 degree heat to the infamous Ramparts division headquarters, the current symbol for the systematic brutality and corruption of the LAPD. It was an odd scene. The Ramparts division building was wrapped in a blue sheet of plastic, as if Christo had stopped by in a somber mood. There's an ATM sign above the steps of the building. "They put that cash machine in there to suggest that it's the only safe place to withdraw money around here," a resident explained. "What happens when you leave the building? They don't say shit about that."

We passed up the Convention the next afternoon in favor of a trip to Simon Rodia's Watts Towers, now in the final months of a five-year rehab program. The five towers, two of them soaring a hundred feet into the air over the misery of the Watts ghetto in south-central Los Angeles, are as glorious as ever. We'd never fully appreciated that one of the main railroad commuter lines from Long Beach to Downtown LA ran along the west side of Rodia's property line and that therefore in the thirty-four years that Rodia worked on his towers between 1921 and 1955 his was most certainly one of the best attended artistic projects in our history. Day after day thousands of commuters saw this tiny man toiling on his great work, often perched 90 feet above the ground wiring the iron struts together or applying mortar and broken china. These days the railroad has gone, as have the trolley cars, and the motorists on the Century and Harbor freeways can't see the Towers.

If Rodia started a similar project today he wouldn't get higher than ten feet off the ground before the Building

Department hit him with a demolition order. As things are it was a close shave for the Watts towers back in 1959 when the Building and Safety Department declared them to be unsafe structures. By now Rodia had moved to northern California, his house had been burned to the ground by vandals. When Kenneth Ross, general manager of the Department of Municipal Arts asked the heads of the Building Department what they would do with the Leaning Tower of Pisa if it was located in LA the bureaucrats answered without hesitation that they would declare them to be unsafe and recommend their demolition. But the bureaucrats were outmaneuvered. Defenders of the Towers organized a load test, in which a winch truck applied 10,000 pound pull on the Towers and succeeded only in bending its own equipment. Amid the cheers of the crowd the head of the Building and Safety Department handed over the red "unsafe" sign to the Defenders. The innate engineering skills of the Italian immigrant had triumphed.

If the Democratic liberals inhabiting the Staples Center, had any sense of drama or history they would have held their own convention in some abandoned lot within eyesight of the Watts Towers. That would have been a declaration of faith in the human spirit. But they sat in the Staples Center and listened to Al Gore, giving his dull imitation of Bill Clinton's State of the Union addresses as devised by Dick Morris. Gore kissed Tipper and trudged his way through the laundry list of items designed to appeal to the middle class. He scored big. The joke came when the commentators termed this a "populist" oration. Gore's poll-driven rhetoric had the same relationship to populism as Kool-Aid to Chateau Lafite.

Everything turned out okay for the Democrats in the end. Al Gore got his post-convention bounce in the polls. Hollywood unbelted millions for the Democratic National Committee. Bill Clinton raised a few bucks for his library. But mostly it was an opportunity for the LAPD to show what life will be like in the police state just around the corner. "Round the corner" is actually an optimistic way of putting it. The police state is here.

Once in a generation you can catch the ruling class off guard. Then you spend the next twenty years paying for it. In Seattle, at the start of December last year, the Direct Action Network, the Ruckus Society and other organizers out-maneuvered the cops and shut the World Trade Organization down. By the time these same demonstrators got to Washington DC the following April, the state had pulled itself together.

One time, walking along a sidewalk opposite the Staples Center we could hear the roar of motorcycles and an instant later saw an elderly woman scuttling away from the center of the sidewalk, just in time to avoid the first of some forty motorcycle cops, two abreast, hurtling along this crowded pedestrian alley at some 40 miles an hour, horns blaring. No demonstration was in progress at the time. It was purely a cop statement from the uniformed and helmeted bikers in blue, "We rule." They did rule, and even with the small and almost entirely peaceful demonstrations that did occur, it's amazing the cops didn't kill someone.

Civil libertarians did score some victories. They got a judge to forbid the planned police shut down of the "convergence center" used as hq by the demonstrators. There will be some civil suits against the cops, one of them filed by the photographer who had his ear torn. But even if they are successful these suits won't slow the trend towards the violent criminalization of all protest, which is the mission of police states down the ages.

What LA was about, in the end, was a continuity of resistance and dissent. Organized labor and the Sierra Club were absent, but here were all the others: the loosely knit of greens, peace activists, farm workers, public transportation advocates, working people angered at anti-labor free trade pacts, gays, lesbians and AIDs activists, death penalty opponents, and dozens of other groups and movements that collectively challenged Gore's Democratic Party. Democrats and the Republicans ignore what's happening in the streets at their own peril. Few seemed to get this. One that does is Rep. Cynthia McKinney from Georgia, who said her heart was with the people in the streets. "I commend today's 'street warriors' for standing up for what they believe in, and knowing that civic engagement is the American way. Let us all do our part to engage and create positive and progressive, social, economic, and environmental change. We need global justice or else 'Workers of the World Unite!' will become more than just a hackneyed slogan; it'll become the only way to survive."

Chapter 6

The Jackboot State

The first glimpse the world had of America's new militarized police was in the news footage and photographs from the Battle of Seattle, images that recurred throughout 2000 in Washington DC, Philadelphia, and Los Angeles. But these storm troopers have been on the streets for more than a decade, wreaking havoc and abusing citizens in the name of the drug war. Call it the Jackboot State or the Prosecutorial State. Either way, the Bill of Rights is fast disappearing, restrictions on the role of the military in domestic affairs have been thrown overboard, all the appurtenances of a police state are in place. Thirty years after the war ended in Vietnam we see what happened when that war came home. We lost abroad. We've lost at home.

For many black Americans and Hispanics the behavior of the cops in Seattle came as no surprise. They've been putting up with thuggish cop tactics such as no-knock forcible entries by heavily armed cops or INS agents for decades. On the religious right, fears about the onrush of tyranny hardened into certainty back at the time of Waco, in the dawn of the Clinton era.

Until recently the liberal-left had been relatively complaisant about the modern police state, preferring to watch re-runs of the McCarthy hearings of the 1950s, while remaining indifferent to Waco or Ruby Ridge. The rampages of special prosecutor Kenneth Starr did perturb them, but mostly because Starr was chasing a Democrat. The behavior of the cops in Seattle and Washington DC came as a wake-up call.

Here's how Sam Smith, longtime Washington reporter and editor of The Progressive Review evoked the events unfolding in the capital in April, 2000: "Illegal sweep arrests. Print shops intimidated into closing by police. Universities canceling public forums under pressure from officials. Homes of opposition leaders broken into and ransacked. Headquarters of the opposition raided and closed by police. These were the sort of things by which we defined the evil of the old Soviet Union. These were some of the reasons we said we had to bomb Yugoslavia. And now they have become characteristics of the federal government's handling of the current protests."

What happened in Washington was a replay of similar cop mayhem in Seattle last December. It's now emerged that a big factor in cop violence was the US Army's Delta Force, whose presence in Seattle was a clear violation of the Posse Comitatus Act of 1887, forbidding the US military any role in domestic law enforcement. This ban is increasingly a dead letter. The Delta Force was at Waco and came to Seattle under the pretext that there might be terrorist biological assaults. As the Seattle Weekly reported, "Using high tech equipment, the Force mapped out potential problem areas as well as identified possible violent demonstrators. Some Deltas wore lapel cameras, continuously transmitting pictures of rioters and other demonstrators to a master video unit in the motel command center, which could be used by law enforcement agencies to track suspects." The Weekly's Rick Anderson quoted a former Delta Force team member as saying, "These guys are the army hotshots, the cowboys. They were wigged out about security here. They thought something drastic had to be done. I'd say they got heard."

In other words, a secret Army unit spied on US citizens on US soil and dictated police tactics to an intimidated local police force which promptly declared the civilian equivalent of martial law in downtown Seattle, suspending civil liberties. It should be added that both in Seattle and Washington, the treatment of arrested people (some of them tourists swept up in the cop rampage) made for hair-raising reading, with random beatings, denials of food and water for 24 hours, racial abuse, threats of rape, refusals to allow consultations with attorneys. As in the 1960s white middle class demonstrators are learning what happens to poor people all the time.

Philadelphia witnessed even deeper intrusions into constitutional protections against police abuses. During the protests at the Republican National Convention in early August, police commissioner John F. Timoney repeatedly denied to the press that his cops had engaged in any covert surveillance of demonstrators. His denials led one gullible reporter to proclaim, "It took the RNC protests to redeem the reputation of the Philly police." But Timoney was lying. His department, working in concert with the state police and the feds, had indeed spied on protesters, intercepted electronic communications, infiltrated their meetings and affinity groups, manufactured search warrants. Even city building inspectors were called upon to use phony charges to shut down buildings where activists were staying or working. All in an effort to disrupt political protests that had been permitted by the City. Of course, Timoney needed to twist the truth to the press, because a 1987 Philadelphia mayoral order prohibits his department —- shamed by so many unconscionable acts against Philly citizens in the past -— from engaging in precisely those kinds of activities.

But finally part of the truth came out. Pennsylvania state police affidavits released nearly two months after the convention revealed that infiltration of the Philly protest groups was based on ludicrous suspicions that... they might be under the control of the former Soviet Union! "Funds allegedly originate with Communist and leftist parties and from sympathetic trade unions", the state police affidavit declared. "Other funds reportedly come from the former Soviet-allied World Federation of Trade Unions."The state police later claimed that the allegations in the affidavit had been fed to them "at no cost, via email" by the Maldon Institute, which police spokesman, Jack Lewis, described as a "private organization that provides intelligence to police departments. Lewis said the Maldon Institute was located "in the United Kingdom". In fact, the puny Maldon Institute makes its home in Baltimore, Maryland, where it is largely underwritten by that tireless promoter of the wacko right, Richard Mellon Scaife.

The scurrilous affadivit based on the Maldon Institute's paranoid fantasies was also used by the cops to justify a search warrant and raid on a building at 4100 Haverford Avenue, in West Philadelphia. The building, an artist's studio, was being used as a puppet-making warehouse for the street protests. The search warrant falsely claimed that the puppet factory was an arsenal containing "weapons and elements of destruction". These charges were made by four men who had shown up at the puppet warehouse to offer their aid. They told the puppet makers that they were members of the Carpenter's Union, recently laid off as stage hands in Wilkes Barre, Pennsylvania. The men were welcomed and put to work. "They were burly, but they didn't seem much like union people or very political", said Adam Eidinger, a publicist who was working at the warehouse. They weren't. The men were, in fact, members of the Pennsylvania state police. They helped orchestrate the police raid on the warehouse that resulted in 75 arrests of puppet makers and activists, the destruction of the puppets and seizure of thousands of dollars worth of personal property. No weapons were found.

Over that week in Philly more than 480 demonstrators were arrested. Three of the leaders were specifically targeted: John Sellers of the Ruckus Society, Kate Sorenson of the Direct Action Network and Terrence McGuckin of the gay rights group ACT UP. None were caught in the commission of any crime. Sellers was nabbed strolling down a sidewalk. They were slapped with an unprecedented $1 million bail on misdemeanor charges of attempted property destruction and criminal conspiracy. Others were held on as much as $500,000 bail. The outrageous bail was a heavy-handed attempt to keep the leaders of the protest off the streets of Philly and from getting to Los Angeles for the Democratic convention two weeks later.

"The nightshift guards tended to be the most sadistic," said a jailed protester named Mali. "Women from the cell block later recalled guessing what time it was according to how many people were hog-tied or hobbled. Since you can't be arraigned if you're naked, many prisoners resisted the system by stripping and going limp when guards came to take them somewhere. The holding cell had windows onto the area where people were fingerprinted and photographed, and we saw our brothers and sisters dragged around naked. The guards didn't like non-compliance too much…We had up to nine women in my [5'x7' cell]. We'd be defecating with someone literally at our knee. We curled up together beside the toilet on the hard with our rank shoes as pillows…Thursday August 3, at 10 PM, our whole cell block managed to unite with the men to all flush our toilets at the same time as George W. Bush was coronated at the RNC."

Tales of police and jail guard torture abounded: verbal abuse, sexual assaults, beatings, shockings with stun guns, withholding of water and bathroom privileges. According to Mali: "People were held up against the wall by their neck until they turned blue, fingers bent back, nipples twisted. One man had his penis twisted by a female guard. Someone heard an officer who was crying say, 'I'm about to throw down my badge and walk out of here.'"

Across the past 30 years both Democrats and Republicans have eagerly colluded in militarizing the police, extending police powers and carving away basic rights. Very often the Democrats have been worse. It was Rep Henry Hyde of Ohio who led the recent and partially successful charge against asset seizure. It was Senator Charles Schumer of New York who was the factotum of the US Justice Department in trying to head off Hyde and his coalition. It was Hyde who in 1997 put into law a measure allowing victims wrongfully prosecuted by the feds to recover attorneys' fees and other costs. Reno's Justice Department fought the bill tooth and nail, and managed to limit the time in which such an action could be filed to 30 days, with no sanctions against those committing the abuses.

Here are some milemarkers in the march of the Jackboot State. (An excellent series in the Pittsburgh Post-Gazette in November of 1998 called "Win At All Costs" stiff offers one of the best surveys of government prosecutorial misconduct.) In 1974 Congress okayed sting operations in which federal agents could create criminal enterprises to trap their targets. These rapidly became forays in entrapment of innocent people fingered by prison snitches trying to get their sentences reduced. In 1989 US Attorney General Dick Thornburgh issued a memo decreeing that federal prosecutors are not bound by ethics rules in the geographic areas where they work. Attorney General

Reno confirmed the rule in 1994. In 1998 a bill pushed through by Reps John Murtha and Joseph McDade repealed it. The Federal forfeiture statutes in 1990 led to widespread abuses which Congress recently tried to curb. In 1984 Congress undercut the exclusionary rule which barred evidence obtained in violation of the Fourth Amendment. Such evidence is now allowed if officers believed in good faith they acted properly. Ha ha. People rot in jail awaiting trial, making the constitutional guarantee of a speedy trial a macabre joke.

Since 1987 police can get a search warrant on the word of an informant who does not even have to be named. Three years earlier, the Supreme Court said evidence obtained through a search warrant not supported by probable cause is admissible so long as it was issued by a "detached and neutral magistrate". Justice John Paul Stevens, in a dissent, said this spelled the destruction of the Fourth Amendment's guarantee against unreasonable searches and seizures.

One of the worst assaults on freedom was the Counter-Terrorism and Effective Death Penalty of 1996 curtailing the right of defendants to appeal, allowing the government to decree what is a terrorist organization and making it a felony to support legal activities of any group linked to any such-designated terrorist organization. The same act permitted the use of undisclosed and illegally obtained evidence against aliens in the US, and allowed them to be deported on such a basis. This act also greatly expanded wiretaps, including those established without a court order.

In 1987 Congress switched the authority for sentencing a criminal defendant from the judge to the prosecutor, by establishing mandatory sentencing guidelines based on the nature of the offense (which of course is chosen by the prosecutor). In 1987 the US Sentencing Commission cut the time to be deducted from a prisoner's sentence for good behavior to a maximum of 54 days a year. This rapidly led to an explosion of lying in court by prisoners desperately looking for reduction in sentences from prosecutors.

Former Attorney General and Supreme Court Justice Robert H. Jackson said, "The [federal] prosecutor has more control over life, liberty and reputation than any other person in America." That was in 1940. With RICO conspiracy laws, money laundering edicts and the like, the situation is far worse today. Discovery: every day across America prosecutors illegally deny defense lawyers evidence that might help establish innocence. Perjury: prosecutors routinely connive at it as their witnesses get leniency in return for testimony. The 12-person jury, cornerstone of our liberties, is routinely undercut and abused by arrogant judges. The misuse of the grand jury by prosecutors is among the most egregious abuses of all.

The insane drug war has been a bipartisan affair. Its consequences are etched into the fabric of our lives. Just think of drug testing, now a virtually mandatory condition of employment, even though it's an outrageous violation of personal sovereignty, as well as being thoroughly unreliable. Of America's two million prisoners, around a third are non-violent drug offenders, with two-thirds of that number being in for marijuana-related offenses. In the era when America was led by two self-confessed pot smokers — Clinton and Gore — the number of cons held on drug crimes in federal prisons has increased by 64 per cent.

No-knock raids are becoming more common as federal, state and local politicians and law enforcement agencies decide that the war on drugs justifies nullifying the Fourth Amendment. As Charles Patrick Garcia noted in a 1993 Columbia Law Review article, "Seven states, favoring strong law enforcement, have chosen a 'blanket approach', which holds that once police have established probable cause to search a home for drugs, they are not required to follow the constitutional knock-and-announce requirement." Even liberal states are jumping on the no-knock bandwagon. The Wisconsin Supreme Court ruled in February, 2000, that police could forcibly enter a home without knocking in any case in which there was "evidence of drug dealing". Unfortunately, "evidence of drug dealing" can be the uncorroborated assertion of a single anonymous paid government informant. The Wisconsin court said that the "possibility for violence" can be minimized by allowing police to rely on "unannounced, dynamic entry" — though it's a good bet that the judges don't expect police to carry out such raids in the judges' neighborhoods.

Even in states where search warrants require a knock on the door before entry, police routinely disregard this formality. In a 1991 corruption trial, a former Los Angeles policeman testified that the accused officers falsely reported that they had complied with the knock-and-announce rule. In reality they violated the rule in 97 percent of the search warrants they executed. No knock raids in response to alleged narcotics violations presume that the government should have practically unlimited power to endanger some people's lives in order to control what others ingest. The right to batter down a door apparently includes the right to kill any citizen who tries to stop the police from forcibly entering his or her home.

As a result of both federal and local actions, America is moving towards the normalization of paramilitary forces in law enforcement. For example, the police in Fresno, California, have taken a big step towards militarization of local law enforcement. The Fresno SWAT team, in full battle gear, now deploys a full-time patrol unit in the city. Deeming the SWAT patrol an "unqualified success", the Fresno police department "is encouraging other police agencies to follow suit". About 90 percent of police departments in cities over 50,000 in population have already put their own paramilitary units into street police work. The same is true in 70 per cent of towns with populations under 50,000. Supplied by the military with a vast array of lethal weaponry (grenade launchers, armored personnel carriers, M-16 rifles, automatic weapons with laser sights, laser surveillance equipment, wireless electric stun projectiles, pyrotechnic devices such as flash bang and smoke grenades, and kevlar body armor) these SWAT teams now often kill unarmed citizens. In Modesto in September, 2000, a police officer in a SWAT team raiding a house told an 11-year old boy to lie on the ground. The boy did so and then was torn apart by a shotgun shell as the edgy cop fired his weapon. In 1990, 62 people died at the hands of the police, while in the first nine months of 1998 the number had grown to 205, an increase of more than 230 percent.

Street deployment of paramilitary units is funded by "community policing" grants from the federal government. The majority of police departments use their paramilitary units to serve "dynamic entry" search warrants. SWAT teams also get deployed in missions very foreign to ordinary police work. The SWAT Team in Chapel Hill, NC conducted a large-scale crack raid of an entire block in a predominantly African-American neighborhood. The raid, termed "Operation Redi-Rock", resulted in the detention and search of up to 100 people, all of whom were African-Americans. (Whites were allowed to leave the area.) No one was ever prosecuted for a crime.

The major cause of the militarization of American law enforcement has been the War on Drugs. In 1981 and 1988, Congress created massive exceptions to the Posse Comitatus Act, to allow use of the armed services, including the National Guard, in drug law enforcement. Every region of the United States now has a Joint Task Force staff in charge of coordinating military involvement in domestic law enforcement. A 1993 JTF Operational Support Planning Guide enthused, accurately, that "Innovative approaches to providing new and more effective support to law enforcement agencies are constantly sought, and legal and policy barriers to the application of military capabilities are gradually being eliminated." Consistent with the trend noted by the JTF, the 1995 session of Congress saw a proposal to create a 2,500 member federal Rapid Deployment Force for the Attorney General to deploy at her discretion to assist local law enforcement.

There are signs of popular unrest and mutiny. The ACLU and the National Rifle Association have jointly called for President Clinton to appoint a commission to investigate "Lawlessness in law enforcement". States with democratic processes such as ballot initiatives have seen brave efforts to curb the War on Drugs. California has a medical marijuana law and Hawaii's legislature just passed one. Oregon and Arizona have also moved to decriminalize personal use. The feds' reaction has been to attack these states by threatening to withhold highway funds, the usual mode of persuasion. Right now the swelling police state is an expression of the War on Drugs. No politician that does not call for a cease fire and a rollback in that cruel futile war — our domestic Vietnam — has any standing to bewail the loss of our freedoms. Those who gasp in amazement at the behavior of the police at demonstrations such as those in Seattle, Washington, Philadelphia and Los Angeles should realise that they entering in the middle of a long, dark story, and that rolling back the Jackboot State here at home is as important as battling the WTO worldwide. It's the same struggle.

Chapter 7

What Are We Fighting For?

Beyond the wildest hopes of the street warriors, five days in Seattle brought one victory after another. Protesters initially shunned and denounced by the respectable "inside strategists", scorned by the press, gassed and bloodied by the cops and national guard: shut down the opening ceremony; prevented Clinton from addressing the WTO delegates at Wednesday night gala; turned the corporate press from prim denunciations of "mindless anarchy" to bitter criticisms of police brutality; forced the WTO to cancel its closing ceremonies and to adjourn in disorder and confusion, without an agenda for the next round.

In the annals of popular protest in America, these were shining hours, achieved entirely outside the conventional arena of orderly protest, white paper activism and the timid bleats of the professional leadership of big labor and establishment greens. This truly was an insurgency from below in which all those who strove to moderate and deflect the turbulent flood of popular outrage managed to humiliate themselves.

The contradiction between the demure agenda of the genteel element and the robust, tear it all down approach of the street legions was already apparent by Tuesday.

Here's a might-have-been. All day long, Tuesday, November 30, the street warriors in downtown Seattle, hopefully awaited reinforcement from the big labor rally taking place around the space needle, some fifteen or twenty blocks from downtown.

But the absent legions of labor never showed. Suppose they had. Suppose there had been 30,000 to 40,000 protesters around the convention center, vowing to keep it shut down all week. Would the cops have charged such a force? Downtown could have been held all night, and perhaps President Bill would have been forced to make his welcoming address from SeaTac or from the sanctuary of his ardent campaign funder, the Boeing Company. That would have been a humiliation for imperial power of historic proportions, like the famous greeting the Wobblies organized to greet president Woodrow Wilson after the breaking of the Seattle general strike in 1919. Workers and their families lined the streets, block after block, standing in furious silence as the President's motorcade passed by. Wilson had his stroke not long thereafter.

This might-have been is not posed out of churlishness, but to encourage a sense of realism about what is possible in the struggle against the trading arrangements now operative in the WTO.

Take organized labor, as embodied in the high command of the AFL-CIO. As these people truly committed to the destruction of the WTO? Of course they aren't. Labor might huff and labor might puff, but when it comes to the WTO what labor wants, in James Hoffa's phrase, is a seat at the table.

In Seattle Big Labor called for a "working group" — a bit of face-saving, actually — which, on the WTO's schedule at that time, wouldn't be up and running till at least 2014AD.

There are unions — the Autoworkers, Steelworkers, Teamsters, Machinists, UNITE — which have rank and file members passionately concerned about "free trade". But how many of these unions are truly ready to break ranks and holler Death to the WTO? For that matter, how many of them are prepared to think in world terms, as the capitalists do? Take the Steelworkers, the only labor group which, in the form of the Alliance for Sustainable Jobs and the Environment, took up position in downtown that Tuesday morning (and later fought with the cops and endured tear gas themselves). But on that same day, November 30, the Moscow Tribune ran a story reporting that the Clinton administration had effectively stopped all cold-rolled steel imports from Russia by imposing penalty duties of 178 per cent. Going into winter those Russian working families at Severstal, Novolipetsk and Magnitogorsk were facing tougher times than ever. The Moscow Tribune's report, John Helmer, wasn't in doubt why: "Gore must try to preserve steel company and steel worker support."

Labor came out of Seattle and headed into a Bash China campaign, hoping to keep China out of the WTO. Some greens also opposed China's entry, fearing that an expanding Chinese economy would fuel CO_2 emissions which (a very debatable scientific proposition) would increase any trend to global warming. In other words, deny China economic development.

As internationalists, we shouldn't be caught in a debate whose terms we don't set, and whose premises are forced on us. James O'Connor put this very well in an editorial in his journal *Capitalism, Nature, Socialism,* written right after Seattle. "Boeing workers might say, 'we're not against industrialization in China or anywhere else but we're the ones who suffer the bad consequences of technology transfer, and we refuse to.' The internationalist rejoinder: 'you don't have to absorb the entire loss yourselves; join us and we can spread the loss over society as a whole via higher unemployment benefits, better job retraining programs, and government-assisted green investment.'... If labor sides with Boeing et al., it's against a redistribution of technology and capital to China; if internationalists side against Boeing and friends, they side with Southern elites against Northern labor."

So we have to stake out our own ground, which is not always that of organized labor in North America which as a matter of self-interest seeks limits to the internationalist effort to redistribute wealth, and also limits to the struggle to redefine wealth in human and natural ecological terms. As O'Connor puts it, "The internationalist struggle to redistribute wealth from capital to labor, rich to poor, North to South, and so on is a 'red moment' of internationalist practice; the internationalist 'green moment' is the struggle to subordinate exchange value to use value and to create ecological societies. The red moment is the quantitative side of things, the green moment the qualitative side."

There's no such thing as "free trade". The present argument is not about trade, for which (except for maybe a few bioregionialists in Ecotopia) all are in favor in some measure. One can denounce General Electric and still be in favor of electricity. The argument is about how trade is to be controlled, how wealth is to be made and distributed. The function of the WTO is to express in trade rules the present balance of economic power on the world held by the big corporations, which see the present WTO round as an opportunity to lock in their gains, to enlist its formal backing in their ceaseless quest for cheap labor and places to dump their poisons.

So ours is a worldwide guerrilla war, of publicity, harassment, obstructionism. It's nothing simple, like the "Stop the War" slogan of the 1960s. Capitalism could stop that war and move on. American capitalism can't stop trade and survive on any terms it cares for.

We truly don't want a seat at the table to "reform" trade rules, because capitalism only plays by the rules if it wrote those rules in the first place. The day the WTO stipulates the phase-in of a world minimum wage of $3 an hour is the day the corporations destroy it and move on. Anyone remember those heady days in the 1970s of the New World Economic Order when third world countries were going to get a fair shake for their commodities? We were at a far more favorable juncture back then, but it wasn't long before the debt crisis had struck, the NWEO was dead and the mildly progressive UN Commission on Trade and Development forever sidelined.

Publicity, harassment, obstructionism...Think always in terms of international solidarity. Find targets of opportunity. South Africa forces domestic licensing at cheaper rates of AIDS drugs. Solidarity. The Europeans don't want bio-engineered crops. Fight on that front. Challenge the system at the level of its pretensions. Make demands in favor of real free trade. Get rid of copyright and patent restrictions and fees imposed on developing nations. Take Mexico. Dean Baker, of the Center for Economic and Policy Research reckons that Mexico paid the industrial nations in 1999 $4.2 billion in direct royalties, fees and indirect costs. And okay, let's have real free trade in professional services, with standardization in courses and tests so that kids from Mexico and elsewhere can compete with our lawyers, accountants and doctors.

The truth about capitalism, as O'Connor remarks, "is that trade and market competition are the ways that property owners overcome society's taboo against theft." Our anti-WTO movement opposes the very definition of capitalism as a 'market economy', which destroys human culture and community, exploits labor and degrades nature. The WTO is the mouthpiece of neoliberalism, an outlook and an economic philosophy that finds radical democracy equality intolerable. So, justice in world trade is by definition a revolutionary and utopian aim. Let's get on with it.

WHY WE FOUNDED COUNTERPUNCH

By Alexander Cockburn and Jeffrey St Clair

Seven years ago we felt unhappy about the state of radical journalism. It didn't have much edge. It didn't have many facts. It was politically timid. It was dull. So we founded CounterPunch. We wanted it to be the best muckraking newsletter in the country. We wanted it to take aim at the consensus of received wisdom about what can and cannot be reported. We wanted to give our readers a political roadmap they could trust.

Seven years later we stand firm on these same beliefs and hopes. We think we've restored the honor of muckraking journalism in the tradition of our favorite radical pamphleteers, Edward Abbey, Peter Maurin and Ammon Hennacy, Appeal to Reason, Jacques René Hébert, Tom Paine and John Lilburne.

Every two weeks CounterPunch gives you jaw-dropping exposés on: Congress and lobbyists; the environment; labor; the National Security State.

"CounterPunch kicks through the floorboards of lies and gets to the foundation of what is really going on in this country," says Michael Ratner, attorney at the Center for Constitutional Rights. "At our house, we fight over who gets to read CounterPunch first. Each issue is like spring after a cold, dark winter."

Sign me up for CounterPunch:

❏ $40 one year ❏ $75 two years ❏ $30 low income ❏ $100 institutions

Please send subscription to:

_____

_____

_____

CounterPunch PO Box 228 Petrolia, CA 95558
Call 1-800-840-3683 to subscribe by credit card.

Waiting for Tear Gas

[white globe to black]

In photographing the Seattle demonstrations my working idea was to move with the flow of protest, from dawn to 3 a.m. if need be, taking in the lulls, the waiting and the margins of events. The rule of thumb for this sort of anti-photojournalism: no flash, no telephoto lens, no gas mask, no auto-focus, no press pass and no pressure to grab at all costs the one defining image of dramatic violence.

Later, working at the light table, and reading the increasingly stereotypical descriptions of the new face of protest, I realized all the more that a simple descriptive physiognomy was warranted. The alliance on the streets was indeed stranger, more varied and inspired than could be conveyed by cute alliterative play with "teamsters" and "turtles."

I hoped to describe the attitudes of people waiting, unarmed, sometimes deliberately naked in the winter chill, for the gas and the rubber bullets and the concussion grenades. There were moments of civic solemnity, of urban anxiety, and of carnival.

Again, something very simple is missed by descriptions of this as a movement founded in cyberspace: the human body asserts itself in the city streets against the abstraction of global capital. There was a strong feminist dimension to this testimony, and there was also a dimension grounded in the experience of work. It was the men and women who work on the docks, after all, who shut down the flow of metal boxes from Asia, relying on individual knowledge that there is always another body on the other side of the sea doing the same work, that all this global trade is more than a matter of a mouse-click.

One fleeting hallucination could not be photographed. As the blast of stun grenades reverberated amidst the downtown skyscrapers, someone with a boom box thoughtfully provided a musical accompaniment: Jimi Hendrix's mock-hysterical rendition of the American national anthem. At that moment, Hendrix returned to the streets of Seattle, slyly caricaturing the pumped-up sovereignty of the world's only superpower.